Robbing Drug Dealers

NEW LINES IN CRIMINOLOGY

An Aldine de Gruyter Series of Texts and Monographs

SERIES EDITOR

Thomas G. Blomberg, *Florida State University*

Thomas G. Blomberg and Karol Lucken
American Penology
A History of Control

Bruce A. Jacobs
Robbing Drug Dealers
Violence Beyond the Law

Robbing Drug Dealers

Violence Beyond the Law

BRUCE A. JACOBS

Aldine de Gruyter
New York

About the Author

Bruce A. Jacobs
Associate Professor of Criminology and Fellow, Center for Metropolitan Studies, University of Missouri-St. Louis.

ALDINE DE GRUYTER
A divison of Walter de Gruyter, Inc.
200 Saw Mill River Road
Hawthorne, New York 10532

This publication is printed on acid free paper ∞

Library of Congess Cataloging-in-Publication Data

Jacobs, Bruce A. (Bruce Abel), 1968–
    Robbing drug dealers : violence beyond the law / Bruce A. Jacobs.
        p. cm. -- (New lines in criminology)
    Includes biblographical references and index.
    ISBN 0-202-30647-X (cloth : alk. paper) -- ISBN 0-202-30648-8
    (pbk. : alk. paper)
      1. Robbery. 2. Narcotics dealers--Crimes against. I. Title. II. Series.

    HV6652.J33 2200
    364'52--dc21

                                                                00-056983

Manufactured in the United States of America

10 9 8 7 6 5 4 3 2 1

Contents

Preface and Acknowledgments

RATES OF ARMED ROBBERY have been declining steadily for the better part of ten years. Much of the decline has been attributed to decreases in crack use, incapacitation effects from swelling prison populations, and the absorption of offenders into a rapidly expanding U.S. economy (Blumstein and Rosenfeld 1998). Yet some criminologists assert that the decline may, at least in part, be illusory, and that offenders are simply shifting to victims who can't or won't call the police (Johnson, personal communication). Foremost among such targets are drug dealers who, in many ways, represent the perfect victim.

They are visible, accessible, and plentiful. They deal only in cash. Many are targets of their own making—flossing, bragging, or otherwise calling attention to themselves. Others are identified through gossip or inside information. The urban topography provides numerous staging areas from which to attack them. Robberies can be melded with drug purchases, allowing perpetrators to capitalize on the element of surprise. Compliance is secured rapidly and at acceptable risk. Bystanders are reluctant to intervene; on the streets, no one wants to get involved in someone else's troubles. The threat of retaliation is real but can be reduced to tolerable levels. And dealers obviously cannot go to the police to report their victimization.

Despite the widely held assumption that violence is something that happens only (or primarily) to law-abiding citizens, the disproportionate share of criminal victims are themselves involved in crime. Yet extant scholarship has failed to explore the contingencies that mediate offenses such as drug robbery—from the forces that inspire it, to the methods used to select targets, to the means employed to generate compliance, to the tactics used to thwart retaliatory attempts after the crime has ended. Given that predatory behavior between and among offenders ultimately spreads to society writ large (the so-called contagion effect), a research gap of striking proportions has emerged. This book intends to fill this gap, drawing from the accounts of active offenders.

No book ever is written in isolation, and I would like to take this opportunity to thank several persons who have been instrumental in its development and execution. My sincere appreciation goes to Richard Wright for convincing me to take an even tighter focus on armed robbery, and that such a focus would be worthwhile. Richard provided the catalyzing force necessary to get this study up and running, and wrote most of the grant proposal responsible for funding the research. His initial enthusiasm was as contagious as the conflict spirals he kept harping on. Special thanks also go to Volkan Topalli, a vital member of the research team, whose incisive interviewing style brought out nuances in the data I might have otherwise missed. His cool management of volatile informants was invaluable as well; on numerous occasions, Volkan defused combustible situations with a firm and steady hand. Thanks go as well to my esteemed colleagues in the Department of Criminology at the University of Missouri-St. Louis. The manuscript is much better off for the advice, counsel, and criticism offered by Eric Baumer, Bob Bursik, Jennifer Bursik, Scott Decker, Dave Klinger, Janet Lauritsen, Volkan Topalli, and (especially) Rick Rosenfeld and Richard Wright. I am indebted to Laurie Mitchell, transcriptionist extraordinaire, whose ear for street dialect is matched only by her conscientiousness and attention to detail. I also would like to extend my gratitude to Bruce Johnson, whose advice and contacts have proved invaluable, both personally and professionally. As always, thanks go to my loving wife Jennifer for her support and perceptive editorial suggestions, to my parents Lynn and Frank, to my brother and sister (David and Joy), and to my son Noah Benjamin, just for being there. Finally, I would like to thank Richard Koffler, executive editor at Aldine de Gruyter. His openness to a "cold pitch" at the American Society of Criminology's (ASC) annual meeting in Toronto will be forever appreciated. Ultimately, this book would not have been possible without his leadership and guidance.

The research on which this manuscript is based was funded by Grant No. 98-1SDRP from the National Consortium on Violence Research. Points of view or opinions expressed in this book are those of the author and do not necessarily reflect the position of the funding agency. Portions of Chapter 1 were reprinted with permission from *Criminology* (2000) 38:171–98 (Bruce A. Jacobs, Volkan Topalli, and Richard Wright) and Northeastern University Press (Bruce A. Jacobs, *Dealing Crack: The Social World of Streetcorner Selling*, Boston, 1999). Chapter 5 was adapted from *Criminology* (2000) 38:171–98 (Bruce A. Jacobs, Volkan Topalli, and Richard Wright). Segments of this article also appear elsewhere in the book, and are again reprinted with permission.

CHAPTER ONE

Researching Drug Robbery

with Richard Wright

EW SOCIAL SETTINGS are more perilous than the world of
street-corner drugs. Burns and rip-offs are taken-for-granted
features of the scene. Exploiting others for material gain is
to be expected in a context systematically organized around mutual predation (Jacobs 1999:66). Robbing drug dealers figures
prominently. Their allure as targets is not difficult to fathom. They
are plentiful, visible, and accessible. They deal strictly in cash and
tend to have lots of it; drug selling is a high-volume, repeat business. Their merchandise is valuable, portable, and flexible; it can
be used, sold, or both. They often wear clothing and jewelry with
considerable monetary worth and greater trophy value; on the
streets, filched property enhances the taker's status (Anderson
1999:30, 75). Drug sellers cannot rely on bystanders to come to
their aid; operative norms dictate that witnesses mind their own
business or suffer the consequences. They have no recourse to the
police either: black market entrepreneurs cannot be "victims"
and therefore lack access to official means of grievance redress.
Drug sellers are scapegoats and held responsible, both rightly
and wrongly, for the wholesale destruction of individuals and
communities alike, which legitimizes them as victims.

1

A widely recognized feature of the urban street scene, drug robberies rarely appear in official crime statistics. This owes largely to their extralegal status. But these offenses are important. They make an enormous contribution to the violent reputation of many high-crime neighborhoods; as many as 50 percent of all drug-related homicides may be a consequence of drug robbery and related forms of predation (see Brownstein et al. 1992). They play a crucial role in shaping the interactional environment within which illicit transactions are conducted. They can fuel *official* rates of serious violence, resulting in injuries or deaths that cannot be covered up. This may trigger a contagion of aggression, whereby widening circles of persons are drawn into emergent conflicts (attempts to settle grievances generate countergrievances and this, in turn, spawns lethal retaliatory cycles; see Blumstein 1995; Tedeschi and Felson 1994). "Imperfect retaliation" may be one consequence—vengeance-driven crimes in which victims seek to restore reciprocity at some innocent third party's expense. The instability that results can have serious and long-term consequences, within drug markets and beyond them.

For all of the studies on street robbery, and there are many (see, for example, Cook 1976; Feeney 1986; Gabor et al. 1987; Katz 1988; Pettiway 1982; Shover 1996; Wright and Decker 1997), none have explored the contextual, situational, and interactional factors that mediate drug robberies. This omission is as glaring as it is understandable. The imprudence of robbing other criminals is widely assumed. Offenders are thought to be armed, organized, and pugnacious. The specter of material loss and reputational damage makes resistance a foregone conclusion. The latter can be particularly intolerable and thereby energize reprisal all by itself: To give in without a fight is to punk out. And to punk out chances the ultimate stigma. Indeed, cowards will find that their criminal careers come to a rapid and ignominious end. In the criminal underworld, there is no place, or mercy, for the weak.

Yet criminologists paradoxically observe that a major benefit of robbing fellow criminals is that they cannot report the offense to authorities (Wright and Decker 1997). The obvious question emerges: Why should offenders elect to reduce their chances of getting arrested at the cost of increasing their odds of being killed? What is it that allows them to accept this putatively greater risk?

The present book aims to address this and related questions, exploring the dynamics that make robbing drug dealers not only acceptable, but preferred. It examines the evolution of the offense—from the forces that inspire it, to the methods used to select targets, to the means employed to generate compliance, to the tactics used to thwart retaliatory attempts after the crime has ended. It investigates the totality of offender decision making, assessing the ways in which motivational factors, situational characteristics, and environmental cues come together in the mind of the criminal to both trigger and shape the offense. It explores the interactional contingencies that swirl around all phases of such crimes, posing and answering a number of important questions. How, for example, does the possession or presence of weapons, actual or perceived, shape the planning and commission of drug robberies? How is victim compliance defined and secured in an inherently dangerous and unstable context? How do spatial, physical, and temporal features of the offending context influence offender decision making? How do fears of victim retaliation enter into the decision-making calculus before, during, and after offenses?

Answers to these questions are situated within a larger phenomenological context. Criminal decision making, after all, does not occur in a vacuum. It is essential to specify precisely how important foreground influences mediate, and are mediated by, offender behavior. The analytic framework applied to do this is a hybrid of rational choice theory and phenomenological interactionism (see Wright and Decker 1994). Both focus on the immediate circumstances relevant to crime and its commission. Both also highlight the situational and sequential nature of criminal decision making (Wright and Decker 1994). Rational choice theory, however, treats the process as a calculated and deliberate one; offenders carefully weigh the costs and benefits of a contemplated act before determining the best course of action. "As such, it stresses the objective factors that shape offenders' decisions . . . " (Wright and Decker 1994:31). Phenomenological interactionism, by contrast, explores "feeling" states as the driving force behind choice. Subjective issues are paramount; crime is a function of emotion and flows of behavior as they interface with ongoing social activity. Combining the two approaches permits the assessment of the dual impact of "hard, verifiable contingencies" (such as risks, rewards, and physical obstacles; Wright and Decker 1994:31) and mood/intuition on emergent conduct. The tensions, dilemmas, and contradictions that result—and their larger implications for order and violence beyond the law—emerge as core concerns of the book. Indeed, chapter 6 concludes the monograph by attempting to resolve them.

A study of drug robbery is urgently needed. Not only could it lead to a better understanding of how cycles of urban street violence are promoted and intensified, it might also suggest critical points of intervention to break these cycles before they spin out of control. The best way to accomplish this is to go to the offenders themselves. They have a unique firsthand perspective of undeniable importance. The book takes a "naturalistic" approach to this end, exploring the offense from the perspective of those who actually commit such crimes (see also Matza 1969).

DRUGS AND CRIME

Drug robbery is situated squarely within the drugs-crime nexus, one of the most powerful and exhaustively studied relationships in all of criminology. Despite some quibbling about causal order, the general consensus is that drug use, especially hard-drug use, succeeds criminal behavior but then intensifies it (see, for example, Ball et al. 1983; Nurco et al. 1981; Shaffer et al. 1985). This intensification most often is attributed to an increasing need to generate large amounts of cash to sustain a habit. Psychopharmacological, economically compulsive, and systemic factors are principally implicated (Goldstein 1985).

Drugs affect mood, resulting in increased excitability, irrationality, and aggressiveness. Consumption becomes very expensive very quickly, inciting users to commit income-generating crimes to maintain (or increase) their levels of use; the heaviest users commit the most offenses, the widest variety, and the most serious of them (Inciardi 1986). Predation and violence, finally, are said to inhere structurally in drug markets. This is a function of chronic disputes over finances, product quality, and turf: individuals who "mess with the money" must pay the consequences; burned customers retaliate lest they be burned again; market share is acquired by seizing it from others. Though legal firms face many of the same dilemmas, they have institutional means available to resolve conflicts. On the streets, the principal means of grievance-redress is violence (Brownstein 2000:47; Maher 1997:196; see also Goldstein 1985; Hughes 1977).

Though the drugs–violence relationship has been investigated less systematically than it perhaps deserves—most studies are correlational and ignore mediating foreground influences as well as situational contingencies (for an example, see Kingery et al. 1992)—it has received substantial scholarly attention nonetheless. Research focused directly on robbers indicates that these offenders use the proceeds from their crimes to support heavy drug use (Feeney 1986; Shover 1996; Tunnell 1992). Of particular interest, Inciardi et al. (1993) found that nearly a quarter of the substance-using offenders in their study had taken drugs from another user by force or threat of force within the previous year, and that more than half of the sample had themselves been victims of a drug robbery. Their research, however, provided little information on the situational and interactional mechanisms that shaped such offenses. Wright and Decker (1997), as part of a larger investigation of armed robbery, interviewed a subset of offenders who targeted drug dealers. Though insightful, their research was more suggestive than anything else—leaving a number of critical gaps in our understanding of the situational and interactional context within which drug robberies are committed.

The bulk of the drugs–violence work is recent, systemically focused (see, for example, Riley 1998), and centered on crack cocaine, a substance that emerged on the street scene circa 1985. Burgeoning demand for this cheap and highly addictive stimulant provoked explosive competition among distributors. Rapid deregulation and turf wars followed (Jacobs 1999a; Johnson et al.

1997). Drug markets underwent wholesale destabilization. Epidemic levels of homicide and assault resulted (Blumstein and Rosenfeld 1998), spurred on by the drug's volatile pharmacology: The crack high is brief, activates a compulsive need for more, and results in an intense, post-use crash. Wanton, often ruthless violence by users is a common consequence (see Maher 1997:56).

Worsening matters, significantly more persons consumed and dealt this drug than ever consumed or dealt heroin or cocaine powder during their respective hey-days (Golub and Johnson 1997a). Large numbers of people were heavy daily users, smoking the substance in copious amounts with unparalleled frequency (Riley 1997). And crack market participants typically conducted transactions in ways that raised their "personal and aggregate risk" (for example, impulsive buying/selling habits, multiple supply sources, large and unregulated dealing networks; see Riley 1998). In combination with widely available firearms, extensive gun-toting, the nonchalant way in which many participants used their weapons, and the dispersion of firearms to persons tangentially involved in the scene, the urban landscape came to mirror the Wild West (for these and other points, see Jacobs 1999a:67). Indeed, the wave of violence associated with crack's emergence is thought to be worse than any previous drug epidemic.

Urban communities were wholly unprepared for the emergent crisis. Formal and informal social controls imploded under the awesome pressure. Out-migration to the suburbs—already robust after years of deindustrialization—accelerated at an unprecedented pace. Social capital disappeared in vacuum-like fashion (Hamid 1998), taking vital economic resources with it. The sweeping destruction of neighborhoods and individuals took on a life of its own. Businesses closed. Housing crumbled. Churches and other stabilizing institutions ceased to hold any restraining influence. Infrastructure disintegrated for lack of upkeep. Once tranquil, law-abiding communities became killing fields into which outsiders wandered at their peril (see Inciardi et al. 1993).

Crack use has now declined and markets have restabilized (Brownstein 1996; Curtis 1999), but drug selling remains a pow-

erfully destructive urban force. A small, but stubbornly recalcitrant number of chronic users persists, served by an equally persistent cadre of hard-core sellers (see Golub and Johnson 1997a
and b). A growing population of marijuana and heroin consumers
is joining the scene. Drug Use Forecasting data indicate that for
the first time in several reporting cycles, the percentage of urban
arrestees testing positive for marijuana is equal to or greater than
those testing positive for cocaine (see, for example, DUF 1997; Cesar 1997a and b). Meanwhile, 320,000 occasional heroin users and
810,000 chronic users were reported nationwide (ONDCP 1996),
up from 136,000 in 1990 and 692,000 in 1992, respectively. Many
have been lured by cheaper, purer, snortable smack perceived to
be safe and nonstigmatizing (see Gervitz 1997; Jacobs 1999b). Urban drug selling thus continues to thrive, and drug robbery remains an attractive offense. Though the illegal standing of drugs
ultimately is responsible for their exaggerated value (the risk of
arrest, theft, injury, and death must be built into their cost; see
Reuter et al. 1990), as well as the exposed status of dealers, this
does not matter. Instability is a fact of life in settings beyond the
law. Drug robbery, one of its primary sources, must be dissected
if meaningful improvements in urban communities are to be
realized.

METHODS

This research draws from the accounts of active drug robbers
operating on the streets of St. Louis, MO.[1] Like other early twenty-
first century rustbelt cities of similar size and type, St. Louis is
foundering. Home to a once vibrant manufacturing sector, it has
become a shell of its former self. Urban decay is firmly entrenched. Opportunities for high-paid work are few and far between. Citizens are fleeing to outlying suburbs in record numbers,
seeking a better life. Difficult-to-replace tax revenue and social
capital are going with them. In the past decade, 15 percent of the
city's population "escaped;" 9,000 residents out-migrated in 1997
alone (Mihalopoulos 1998). St. Louis' small base figure of 340,000

citizens makes the impact terribly acute. The city is developing a concentrated population of the "truly disadvantaged" (Wilson 1987; 1996), people with insufficient resources and substantial social-service needs that cannot be met and are getting worse. Social disorganization is pervasive and provides an ideal context in which drug markets and the violence that permeates them can thrive.

The city's crime rate consistently exceeds that of most U.S. urban locales. In 1999, St. Louis ranked number one in total crimes per capita among American cities with populations larger than 100,000, and fourth in homicides (Hackney et al. 2000). Rates of robbery and serious assault consistently place St. Louis in the top five in the nation (see, for example, FBI 1996); the city's violent crime index recently earned it the shameful distinction of being five times higher than the national average, while its homicide rate came in at six times the national figure (see also Hackney et al. 2000). Increases and decreases in these rates tend to mirror other U.S. cities, albeit at a different scale. This makes St. Louis an ideal laboratory for investigating important correlates of violent crime such as drug robbery (Rosenfeld and Decker 1996).

Historically, St. Louis has had one of the largest and most active illicit drug markets in the midwestern United States. Crack, heroin, PCP, and marijuana are sold openly on many inner-city street corners and are available at virtually any hour. Markets are dominated by freelance sellers—vendors who sell for their own personal profit and who exhibit little in the way of formal organization. Not infrequently, a number of dealers will occupy the same street, corner, or vacant lot at the same time. Though not always blatant, transactions can easily be observed with a modicum of effort. Arrestees persistently have high rates of cocaine-, opiate-, and marijuana-positive urine specimens; they are among the highest of the 35 cities measured in the Arrestee Drug Abuse Monitoring program. Emergency room cases involving cocaine and heroin mirror other large metropolitan areas and indicate a high degree of street-drug institutionalization (see DAWN 1996).

Neighborhoods in which drug markets thrive have all the earmarks of deprivation and decay. Abandoned buildings pockmark the landscape. Litter fills the streets. Bullet-sprayed walls greet visitors and residents alike. Graffiti disclose the most recent victims of urban violence. Misfits young and old collect on the street corner, drinking fortified alcoholic beverages (Cisco, Thunderbird, Night Train), smoking blunts (hollowed out cigars filled with marijuana), looking for action, and more generally, just waiting for something to happen.

DATA COLLECTION

Recruitment

Data from this study were drawn from in-depth qualitative interviews with active drug robbers. Qualitative methods are integral for exploring the conduct of "hidden populations"—groups difficult to reach by virtue of the stigmatizing and / or illegal behaviors its members participate in and actively conceal from outside view (see Spreen 1992). Through such methods, a range of conduct norms, beliefs, and interaction patterns can be documented (information that usually cannot be obtained from official sources). Qualitative methods allow researchers to decode the manner in which subjects (in this case, active criminals) think and act in real-life circumstances, and to describe a body of knowledge or cognition not easily understood by lay persons (Adler 1985; Agar 1973; Johnson et al. 1997). Such methods provide insight into the ways in which offenders interpret, assess, organize, perceive, and classify their social worlds (see Lex 1990:393). A richer understanding of causal relationships pertaining to all facets of experience and process results (Fleisher 1995:21, 104). Finally, qualitative methods document emergent processes—especially vital when those being explored lie at the "forefront of broader trends" that require real-time identification if effective social policy is to be formulated (see Golub and Johnson 1999:1737).

Studying active offenders is difficult precisely because their activity is criminal. Most find it necessary to lead secret lives. This makes them hard to locate. Once located, they are typically reticent to provide valid and reliable information about what it is they do (Irwin 1972:117). Such reluctance should not be surprising.

There are real consequences for indiscretion. Exposure could mean hard time; the more illegal the conduct, the more offenders have to lose if found out. Unremarkably, criminal ethnographers typically are perceived to be undercover agents seeking to obtain damaging evidence for juridical purposes. Indeed, one of the most common suspicions criminals have about field researchers is that they are covert operatives of some sort. As Sluka (1990:115) notes, "It is difficult to find an [ethnographer] who has done fieldwork who has not encountered this suspicion." This belief is perhaps stronger in street-drug markets than in any other setting, as it is a "basic cultural rule . . . to treat everyone as a snitch or the man [police] until proven otherwise" (Agar 1973:26).

Though interviewing institutionalized offenders might be easier, safer, and more efficient, it is not the best way to obtain valid data. Through the ages, criminologists have "suspected that offenders do not behave naturally" in criminal justice settings (Wright and Decker 1994:5). Sutherland and Cressey (1970:68) point out that those who have had "intimate contacts with criminals 'in the open' know that criminals are not 'natural' in police stations, courts, and prisons and that they must be studied in their everyday life outside of institutions if they are to be understood." Polsky (1967:123) is even more emphatic, warning that, "we can [not] afford the convenient fiction that in studying criminals in their natural habitat, we . . . discover nothing really important that [cannot] be discovered from criminals behind bars. What is true for studying the gorilla of zoology is likely to be even truer for studying the gorilla of criminology." Incarcerated criminals may not be representative of the general offender population. Criminologists justifiably assert that those who have been arrested constitute unsuccessful criminals, likely to be different from their uncaught counterparts in some central and/or systematic way (Wright and Decker 1994). Failing to account for this fact can have grave implications for the data one collects and ultimately reports.

Collecting data from predatory offenders, particularly active ones, is likely to be difficult and dangerous unless one can construct friendships within the particular subculture targeted for inquiry. This is arduous, but not impossible. The process can be jumpstarted—which is precisely what we[2] did. Initial respondents were located through the efforts of two street-based African-American field recruiters who had ongoing contacts with our research team. Each recruiter was himself an active member of the criminal underworld. Each also had extensive connections to networks of street offenders and, within those networks, enjoyed a solid reputation for integrity and trustworthiness. As Walker and Lidz (1977:115) remind us, when access to secret worlds is needed, "the individual who will establish the [researcher's] credentials must be well thought of by the other participants in the system." Without the properly located "gatekeeper," research of the type undertaken here has virtually no chance of success.

Trading on their trust, the field recruiters began by approaching relatives, friends, and acquaintances whom they knew to be active drug robbers. They explained our research objectives and told prospective interviewees that they would be paid $50 for participation. It is a cardinal rule of street life that one should never do anything for nothing. Although $50 may seem to be a substantial sum, it is important to remember that most of these offenders could have earned much more through crime. And, from their perspective, crime may have appeared to be less risky than talking to strangers about their formidable law-breaking. Once the field recruiters' initial source of active drug robbers was exhausted, they turned to referrals provided by earlier interviewees to expand the sample further. This "snowball sampling" technique continued until 29[3] drug robbers had been recruited (see also Biernacki and Waldorf 1981 on chain referral).

Perhaps the greatest difficulty encountered by the field recruiters was verifying that potential interviewees met the eligibility requirements for project participation. To be considered an active drug robber, an offender theoretically had to have (1) robbed at least one drug dealer in the last three months, and (2) committed at least three such robberies in the previous year. In practice, however, these criteria sometimes were difficult to apply. Some offenders, whether because of heavy drug consumption, alcohol use, or circumspection, were initially unable or unwilling to recall the necessary information. Careful and sensitive questioning usually overcame this problem but by that time,

the offenders were sitting in front of us; those few who fell slight-
ly outside the inclusion criteria could not safely be sent away
empty-handed, so we interviewed them anyway. From our perspective, this decision made perfect sense. Why turn away potentially valuable informants—individuals who regard themselves
as active drug robbers and who are recognized by other offenders
as active drug robbers—for the sake of adhering to what were,
after all, somewhat arbitrary inclusion criteria in the first place?

The field recruiters at times presented us with problems of their
own. The fact that they were being paid a $50 bounty instead of
a salary kept them under pressure to generate additional interviews in a context where new subject recruitment was difficult
and time-consuming. This, in turn, created a temptation for the
field recruiters to try to deceive us. Early on, one of them brought
in a potential interviewee who looked remarkably similar to
someone we already had spoken to, claiming he was an identical
twin (which he was not). We sent both home with appropriate admonitions. The other recruiter also tried to pass off a former interviewee as a new respondent—crudely bandaging the person's
head, darkening his left eye with mascara, and claiming the individual had been beaten up during a drug robbery. The field
recruiter initially denied involvement in this amateurish dissim-
ulation, but later owned up to his role, admitting that he had
needed money badly that day and had been unable to find a fresh
respondent.

Far from undermining our faith in the field recruiters, such incidents bolstered our confidence that we had chosen them wise-
ly. We hired these individuals because they were known criminals
with a history of exploiting friends and strangers; it would have
been suspicious had they not tried to deceive us. The trick was
not to let them outsmart us by remaining vigilant and approaching each new interviewee with a healthy—if well-hidden—dose
of skepticism.

Beyond trying to deceive us, the field recruiters also attempted
to take advantage of the interviewees by skimming off a portion
of their $50 participation fee. Sometimes they did this openly,
stating that, as agents, they were entitled to a percentage of their
clients' earnings. Other times they tried to resort to subterfuge,

asking us not to pay interviewees directly so that they could ne-gotiate a lower fee with them and pocket the difference. We re-fused to endorse or participate in these schemes, but this did not prevent us from being drawn into disputes. In handling them, we maintained a firm and consistent line; each party was to receive $50 for their services and that was what we were going to pay them. This protected us from charges of favoritism, but it did lit-tle to resolve the disputes themselves. We know through the grapevine, for example, that some of the verbal altercations that erupted in our presence degenerated into fistfights once the dis-putants were on their own again.

Money is the lifeblood of the streets and, as with any precious commodity, disagreements about how available funds should be distributed are to be expected. It would be naive, however, to con-clude that these disagreements had no impact on the process of recruiting potential interviewees. Participants who felt they had been cheated were unlikely to recommend the experience to their associates. We frequently reminded the field recruiters of this fact and, for varying lengths of time, this proved effective in stifling their desire to shortchange interviewees. Inevitably, though, they drifted back into bad habits, especially during periods of finan-cial hardship. This is very much in keeping with the general ethos of streetlife, where everybody is looking for a way to capitalize on someone else's good fortune.

Interviews

The interviews, which typically lasted about an hour, were semistructured, conducted in an informal manner, tape-recorded (with respondents' permission), and transcribed verbatim. Ques-tions focused on the offenders' most recent drug robbery, but al-lowed for sufficient expansion to gauge whether this offense was executed in typical fashion. If it was not, additional questions were asked to determine the offenders' usual modus operandi. Interviewees were allowed to respond freely and to introduce their own concepts and categories. This strategy has been used successfully to generate "thick description" with a wide variety of active criminals, including residential burglars (Wright and Decker 1994), street robbers (Jacobs and Wright 1999) and crack dealers (Jacobs 1999a).

In questioning the offenders, we disaggregated their offenses into a series of closely linked sequential actions: motivation, target selection, enactment, and retaliatory threat management. The value of this basic operational scheme has been demonstrated in previous work; it permits the exploration of objective and subjective aspects of situations that influence offender decision making immediately before, during, and after their crimes (see Wright and Decker 1994).

In the area of motivation, the interview schedule contained questions about the situational and interactional factors that lay behind the decision to commit drug robbery. The role of drug/alcohol use, peer association, and weapon availability was preeminent in this regard. We also explored whether alternative courses of action were pondered. This led to questions intended to identify the unique appeal of drug robbery. Why, we asked, commit this offense as opposed to some other realistically available crime? What are the specific advantages and disadvantages of drug robbery? What makes drug dealers good targets? What role do perceptions of sanction risks play—both formal and, especially, informal—in the decision-making process? Recall that a major allure of robbing drug dealers is that they cannot go to the police, but why should offenders who are rational enough to worry about the risk of arrest be willing to run the much greater danger of injury or death that goes hand in hand with preying on fellow criminals? What is it about these offenders, or the situations in which they find themselves, that makes them amenable to accepting this risk?

Turning to the issue of target selection, the interview schedule contained questions to disclose how and why particular drug dealers were singled out for victimization. What, for example, makes for an attractive victim? Where are they located? How are they found? Which targets are better, solitary ones or those in groups? Is it wise to rob dealers one knows? Why or why not? Are targeted dealers armed? How is this information obtained? Are there other forms of defensibility that mediate target attractiveness? How do temporal issues figure into the selection process?

Physical locations in which dealers ply their trade also play an important role in causing them to be targeted. Thus, we asked offenders about the role of geography in target selection. What, for instance, is the best place to rob a dealer? What features make for an attractive offense site? Are certain areas avoided? Why? What is the relationship between local activity patterns and the selection of drug robbery locations? How does the role of natural surveillance influence the selection process?

In the realm of enactment, we asked offenders directly about the strategies they employed to commit their crimes. How are approaches made without "tipping one's hand" too early? How is compliance generated? How is it made to last the duration of the offense? What happens when such efforts fail? How are non-compliant victims managed? Does the likelihood of recalcitrance vary by the enactment site? If co-offenders are involved, how are their roles defined and delegated? What steps are taken during the offense to avoid identification and to minimize the subsequent possibility of retaliation?

Questions such as these lead naturally to consideration of the aftermath of drug robberies and in particular, about reprisal. How do offenders cognitively and practically handle this threat? Do their movements and activities change? How so? For how long? Does the perceived risk of retaliation decrease over time? Do attempts made to avoid retaliation make offenders more susceptible to formal sanction threats? If so, what makes the trade-off worth it? Despite a good deal of speculation that violence in high-crime urban communities is often retaliatory in nature—representing a rough-and-ready form of street justice—answers to such questions remain obscure.

Validity

Considerable effort was made to question every offender about every issue. Unfortunately, open-ended qualitative interviewing mitigates against universal coverage. Topics frequently emerge later in the process that may not have been anticipated early on (see Henslin 1972:52). Responses did become repetitious, however, which suggested that we were saturating the categories specified in the research protocol. Admittedly, however, such saturation could have been an artifact of the sampling design itself. Even if real, such a flaw need not be damning; imperfections are an unavoidable part of the ethnographic enterprise. As Van Maanen (1988:56–57) reminds us, absent evidence of fallibility, the fieldworker may "appear too perfect and thus strain the reader's good faith" (see also Wright and Decker 1994:23).

The drug robbers in the sample ranged in age from 15 to 46; the mean age was 28.86. All of them were African-American; all but five were male. On average, respondents had completed the 11th grade. Most were unemployed and unmarried at the time they were interviewed. Most claimed to have no particular place of residence. As urban nomads, they roamed from house to house— "crashing" with kin, friends, and sexual partners as the mood struck them. There is no way of knowing how well this sample represents the total population of active drug robbers, but it confidently can be said to over-represent African-American offenders. No doubt the racial composition of our sample reflects the social chasm that exists between African-Americans and whites in the St. Louis criminal underworld. These offender-groups display a marked tendency to "stick to their own kind," seldom participating in overlapping criminal networks. The fact that both of our field recruiters were African-American meant that they had few realistic opportunities to establish bonds of trust with white offenders; they simply had little day-to-day contact with them.

This raises larger questions about external validity. As Maher (1997:29) notes, the "positivist nightmare that research participants, individually or collectively, may not be 'representative' or worse still, that they may be exceptional or idiosyncratic, runs deep." Sampson and Raudenbush (1999:607) elevate this concern to stratospheric heights, claiming it to be a "fundamental cleavage of sociological criminology." The representativeness of a sample drawn from drug robbers at large in the community can never be determined conclusively because the parameters of the total population are unknown (Glassner and Carpenter 1985). Context-specific characteristics of drug markets are likely to vary and, accordingly, so will the motivations, target selection, enactment, and retaliatory threat-management strategies drug robbers use and report. At the same time, readers recognize that traditional methods—such as surveys sent to homes—would not be able to obtain such data; they are inefficient, ill-targeted, and unable to produce respondents in reliable numbers (Heckathorn 1997:174). Yet even if the present sample cannot be generalized to the total population of drug robbers, it can nonetheless broaden our understanding of how such offenders operate in real-life settings and circumstances. The research site—St. Louis—would also seem to provide data relevant to a number of cities of similar type, size, and location. This is important. St. Louis is *not* like Miami, Los Angeles, Chicago, or New York—the loci of so much street drug/crime research—but those cities are themselves unlike many others across the nation.

Concerns about internal validity are perhaps more pressing. Here we were butting into the lives of persons engaged in violent felonies for which they could suffer severe sanctions, both formal and informal. How could we know they were telling the truth? Was it not in their best interest to be mendacious, especially since the possibility of exposure threatened their future success as criminals? A number of respondents were admittedly leery at first, but most relaxed and opened up soon after discussion began. Solid rapport was developed in the vast majority of sessions; interviewees often became lively and quite conversational (see Berk and Adams 1970 on generating rapport with subjects). Many seemed to enjoy speaking with someone "straight" about their lives, as it was a rare opportunity to impart their own brand of street wisdom to putative squares supposedly smarter than them, at least in terms of formal education. Offenders often find this process liberating. As Wright and Decker (1994:26) note, "The secrecy inherent in criminal work means that offenders have few [chances] to discuss their activities with anyone besides associates, a matter which many find frustrating" (see also Letkemann 1973). Offenders almost inevitably have skills and knowledge that researchers lack, and this may empower them to talk more freely about a larger number of issues. Insofar as they see something in the research that benefits them, or define it as an opportunity to correct inaccurate perceptions of what they believe or how they behave, candid replies are correspondingly facilitated.

We attempted to minimize lying and distortion in every way possible. We promised the interviewees complete anonymity and never asked for their real names.[4] We assured them that what they told us would be held in the strictest confidence. We made specific inquiries designed to screen out those who may have been less than forthright. We monitored the truthfulness of their responses by checking for and questioning inconsistent answers. We emphasized the importance of being sincere at every turn; their comments would end up in a book—which impressed many and motivated more to "get it right." We underscored our solid relationship with the field recruiters who referred them; if they said it was safe to disclose privileged information, we hoped that it would be believed.

Drawing from a sample of active street criminals similar to the one included here, Wright and Decker (1994) compared offenders' self reports of arrest to official arrest records. They concluded that previous arrests were not underreported (also, see West and Farrington, 1977). Drug robberies seldom are reported to the police, so we could not check arrest records. That said, numerous opportunities arose during our research to verify that interviewees really were drug robbers and that what they said about their crimes was true. Six of them told us that they had been shot during one of their robberies and backed up this claim by showing us their bullet wounds, some of which were in private places not normally visible to nonintimates. At least two of the offenders brought pistols to their interviews. On several occasions we interviewed two or more offenders who had taken part in the same robbery. Although they were interviewed separately, often weeks apart, their descriptions closely matched.

We also asked one of the field recruiters to sit in on several interviews relating to incidents of which he had direct knowledge. He said little during these interviews, although, on occasion, an interviewee asked him for help in recalling a precise location or exact address—something that we all have done in conversations with acquaintances. After the interviews, we debriefed the field recruiter to gauge the truthfulness of the drug robbers' accounts; in every case, he assured us that the interviewee had given us a broadly faithful description of the offense.

It could be argued that the field recruiters, in an effort to provide criminal acquaintances with easy cash, had somehow coached them to respond in a manner consistent with the goals of the project. In retrospect, this seems highly unlikely. First and foremost, the *specific* substance of the very detailed interview questionnaire was never described to recruiters. Nor were the stated empirical goals of the study. As such, they had no way of instructing interviewees how to respond "appropriately." One also would assume that such coaching would have had to take our inclusion criteria into account (i.e., the recruiters would instruct potential respondents to lie about their eligibility). Yet a small number of respondents freely admitted falling outside these criteria, suggesting that they were not attempting to tailor their responses to our needs. Moreover, if preinterview rehearsal was occurring, we would expect to obtain a rather homogeneous set of responses and descriptions. This was not the case. Respondents described a variety of settings, locations, strategies, and circumstances, providing a diverse array of information not consistent with premade scripts.

Interviewing the victims of drug robbery, to corroborate the drug robbers' claims made here, would have been ideal but was beyond the scope of the present study for practical and logistical reasons. In a forthcoming paper, however, Topalli and Wright (2000) report significant overlap between the two parties' accounts (of both the offenses and the retaliatory aftermath). Importantly, the drug-seller victims they interviewed were recruited from the same St. Louis neighborhoods at roughly the same time that the present research was conducted, using the same recruiters—thereby minimizing the confounding effects of ecology, period, and microstructure.

The validity and reliability of offender self-report data have been carefully assessed by a number of researchers, all of whom conclude that semistructured interviews represent one of the best ways to obtain information about crime (see, for example, Ball 1967; Huizinga & Elliott, 1986). Indeed, the most accurate of such data are said to come from face-to-face interviews—the strategy used here—as opposed to surveys administered by way of phone or mail. This is not to say that offender self-reports are bereft of

"exaggerations, intentional distortions, lies, self-serving rational-
izations, or drug-induced forgetfulness" (Fleisher 1995:80), but
rather, that they may not be as vulnerable to such pitfalls as so
many widely presume. Admittedly, in the absence of actually *seeing* the offenders *do* what it is they talk about (not an option here
for obvious practical and ethical reasons), we can never know
how truthful they are being. Nonetheless, we believe that undetected cases of distortion were sufficiently rare as to not undermine the overall validity of the data.

The book makes extensive use of quoted material from the interview transcripts. Needless to say, such excerpts comprise but
a small part of what offenders actually said. As Wright and Decker (1997:31) observe, "Selectivity is an unavoidable problem in the
textual representation of any aspect of social life—criminal or
otherwise—and it would be naive to claim that this cannot dis-
tort the resulting manuscript." Also unavoidable is drawing disproportionately from the observations of some respondents. In
any project, certain informants will be more helpful, informed,
candid, articulate, or knowledgeable about a particular topic or
process than others (see also Prus 1984:253). Reliance on them is
necessary to get the story "right." Quotes have been appropriat-
ed to capture the essence of the particular theme under investigation, and every effort has been made to represent a wide array
of offenders.

Anecdotes have been edited to meet the textual demands of a
manuscript of this nature. But colorful, sometimes profane language has not been removed; the intention is to provide readers
a better feel for the flavor and jargon of street talk, a vibrant combination of Black English, slang, and drug lexicon (see also Maher 1997:224). Periodically, words or phrases in brackets will
appear. These indicate an attempt on my part to explain and / or
amplify something a respondent has said. The text also is supplemented at times with insights gained during the course of several
years of field research on the consumption, sale, and interdiction
of street drugs—preceding and including the study period—
from individuals and settings relevant to the present topic (cf.
Mieczkowski 1986). Such insights are crucial in providing a more
precise understanding of the broader context in which drug rob-

bers perform their crimes. In qualitative research, the researcher is the research instrument and his or her experiences contextualize the work in important ways (Wright and Stein 1996).

The book is arranged sequentially, consistent with the analytic framework used to anchor and organize the data. Chapter 2 explores the forces that energize the decision to commit drug robbery. Chapter 3 examines the tactics drug robbers use to identify and select suitable targets. Chapter 4 investigates the enactment process—how approaches are made, compliance is generated, and goods transferred. Chapter 5 explores strategies used to manage the threat of retaliation after the offense has been completed. Chapter 6 examines the conceptual implications of drug robbery for order and violence beyond the law.

NOTES

1. The study design, sampling protocol, data collection techniques, and justifications driving their use are similar to those used and discussed by the author and his colleagues in previous work (Jacobs 1998:165, 166–67; Jacobs 1999a:8–13, 22–25; Jacobs 1999b:557–59; Jacobs and Miller 1998:553–55; Jacobs and Wright 1999:151–53; Jacobs, Topalli, and Wright 2000: 173–77). The following methods section draws from that material, with portions reprinted with permission from Northeastern University Press and *Criminology* (please see "Acknowledgments" for more specific citation information).
2. Volkan Topalli, an NSF National Consortium on Violence Research Postdoctoral Fellow, assisted in the data collection process.
3. Actually, we interviewed thirty but one looked so similar to a previous respondent (he reportedly was his older brother) that we merged the two transcripts into one. Though I have very good reason to believe they were indeed separate persons, I could never prove it.
4. Street names, however, were taken and are used throughout the monograph. These names are sufficiently common so as to not jeopardize the anonymity of the respondent to whom they refer. To protect further against possible exposure, proper names of persons that respondents mention in their transcripts have been changed; this is especially important when the individuals concerned are past victims, who may be unaware of the identity of their victimizers (yet be familiar with their street names).

CHAPTER TWO

Motivation

ROBBERY IS ALL ABOUT material gain and few offenses rival the riches promised by drug robbery. Cash seizures can measure in the thousands of dollars, drug hauls in ounces rather than grams. Luxury accessory items (for example, cars, jewelry) are frequently side benefits of heists. The mandates of drug selling require that vendors have large cash and drug reserves on hand. Inventory must be maintained and restocked, lest one lose business in a highly competitive marketplace. This requires liquid currency that cannot be banked without attracting suspicion. One outcome is that sellers regularly end up blowing disposable income on personal, nonessential consumption items. On the streets, the "material trappings of success" (Shover 1996) create the impression of wealth by which everyone is judged.

High-yield crimes are critical for those who burn money as fast as they make it. Drug robbers do precisely that. Theirs is a life driven by the open-ended pursuit of illicit street action. Illegal drug use figures most prominently in their "life as party" (Shover 1996), with the vast majority consuming mind-altering substances in significant quantities at tremendous cost. The urge to use drugs was in many ways beyond their ability to control (Wright and

Decker 1994:40). Indeed, the quest for intoxication was a basic drive—much like hunger, thirst, and sex are for ordinary citizens (see Siegel 1989:10). No amount ever really seemed enough to satiate them. "I got to get high, I got to get high," J Rock pronounced. "That's what I got to do. I got to get high. . . . Nothing to me but getting high, time to get high, time to get high, got to get high." June Bug claimed that $800, an amount which could buy nearly an ounce of crack (about 150 $20 rocks after retail markup) "ain't no money. What is $800 . . . ? You can run through $800 in 45 minutes [using crack]." Others expressed similar sentiments:

> Messing with drugs, you chasing a dream. . . . Fourteen $20 rocks, I did 14, $20 rocks in a pipe last night. . . . Stones I did last night, it's over with, it's history. . . . I want to get me 14 more today and I'm gonna do them today.—*Slim*

> The more [crack] you smoke the more you want. You don't never get enough and you don't never get no high but it's just the taste. You just taste it and you just want to keep getting that, they call it chasing the ghost, that's all you doing, you ain't gonna get no high but it makes you want to keep smoking it. You sit down, you smoke up a fucking pack of cigarettes in about 30 minutes and you ain't got nothing else to smoke you know and you find people looking on the floor. They ain't dropped nothing, what you looking for? He ain't dropped nothing. I don't never know anybody that dropped some. Then he start thinking about where he gonna get some more from.—*Jay*

Lack of cash meant an end to the party, and an end to the party threatened substantial pain. Shortfalls were especially intolerable for those addicted to heroin, a significant portion of the sample. Unlike crack—which foments psychological dependence—heroin quickly becomes necessary to one's physical well-being. Withdrawal is perceived to be acutely traumatic and something to be avoided at all costs. "Once you got a [heroin] habit, man," Curly implored, "you need dope [heroin] all day and everyday . . . that one shot ain't gonna get it. . . . You need dope all day long, 24 hours a day dope, man. You need dope to get up with, you need dope to go to bed with. You can't use the toilet, man, without dope . . . you just fucked up, man. You can't even concentrate right without dope. . . . Your body aches without dope." Getting "fixed" becomes a daily obsession:

> When you constantly get high, you want to get high, high, high, high, high. Your body get immune to it so you want more, more, more.—*Do-dirty*

There is perhaps no better way to relieve intense, immediate, and costly pharmacological cravings than through drug robbery. Widely available, readily accessible, and possessing the precise goods respondents want most, drug sellers represent obvious targets. "I'm a dope fiend," Do-dirty explained. "They got the money and the dope. That's a high, you see what I'm saying. If you got the money and you got the dope, Do-dirty gonna get his." Curly concurred:

> You ain't got no money, you need a fix. You got a pistol. It's some dope in the street. You don't have to make your mind up, your mind already made. You need some dope and the quickest mark you can get. . . .

As funding sources, nondealers simply could not measure up. "What you gonna rob somebody else for?" Baby Doll grumbled. "They could have maybe $10 or $20, that's not much you know. . . . [With drug dealers] you get money, you get the dope, you get jewelry . . . take off with the car, sell the car, sell everything." Blackwell agreed: "Why go rob some old lady when you can just rob a drug dealer and you'll get more?"[1] Even currency-laden retail outlets were perceived to offer an inferior take:

I ain't gonna rob no store. . . . Why would I rob them for and get they little two or three hundred dollars, probably not even that much when I can go hit this dope man for about $5,500, an ounce or something, big birds [kilos] or something, you know, stuff like that, nice big Rolexes and nice big necklaces and diamond rings and all that type of stuff. Why would I go rob a little 7-11 for? They ain't making no money for real, that ain't no money to me, three or four hundred dollars, that ain't no money to me. I like grands, I like big dollars. That little dollars, that ain't nothing, I'll blow that in 30 minutes or something. . . . I like that big money. I like to catch them big ballers with all the dope.—*Smoke Dog*

Loot seized from drug dealers offered the best of possible worlds. As YoYo put it, "You got your dope, you got something to smoke and then you also got some way you can make your money back and keep your stuff going on and on"—implying that she would use at least part of her drug haul to generate additional revenues. Indeed, the ease with which illicit drugs could be converted into cash made the offense enormously enticing (see also Reidel 1993:152); drugs also could serve as currency in their own right. This is to say nothing of the rapidity with which seizures could be made and, as anyone who has ever stumbled upon a $20 bill in the street can attest, rewards earned quickly with little effort often seem larger than they really are. "You are only talking about maybe 90 seconds," Buck mused. "You ain't talking about no time." June Bug said that, "three minutes [and] it's over. It's just [easy]. . . ." Smoke Dog declared that he could "make $300 in ten minutes." K-red explained that "you don't have to do nothing but rob and run." Ray Ray claimed he could "pull a [drug] robbery so quick you never know you been robbed." Or, as Crazy Jack remarked:

I could rob somebody in less than a minute. Once I pull a gun out . . . it be so quick and easy they never know, they thinking they scared I'm gonna do it and I already did it. "Are you ready?" I'm like "it's already done," I already robbed and I'm gone, I already got 'em.

Unlike traditional offenses such as burglary and shoplifting, there were no intermediate steps required to convert stolen goods into currency. The time and effort required to do so is prohibitive for those who want rewards *now* (see also Feeney 1986; Wright and Decker 1997; Maher 1997:116; Koester and Schwartz 1993). "What's the sense of [stealing home electronics]?" Ray Ray asked. "I don't feel like walking around trying to sell no TV or VCR, none of that stuff. I want strictly cash money in my hand." Do-dirty agreed: "Man, I ain't gonna be trying to break in no house, ain't gonna be trying to sell no stuff. I'm gonna go where the money at." Ray Dog and Slim echoed similar sentiments:

> Burglary, its not what I want. One thing about the burglary, you got to wait, get it, then you got to find someplace to sell it. Robbing a dope dealer, you ain't got to worry about selling, going and finding a place to sell it. You just go out and get the money, get the dope. . . . I'm cool on robbing, I love it man; they sweet, they sweet, man; I'm telling you, they sweet. . . .
>
> I don't do burglaries, I don't do no shoplifting, too big of a cause. Why would I go in the store trying to pick up maybe four, five, six items that maybe cost $150 apiece that I might come out here on the streets and I might sell them for $75 apiece? . . . All I got to do is catch this little boy [dealer] over here and do what I got to do and get easy money.[2]

Securing funds through lawful employment obviously was not an option. Most respondents lacked the education, skills, and so-cial capital necessary to obtain legitimate work at a level suffi-cient to sustain their cash-intensive lifestyle. The jobs open to them were menial and poorly remunerated. Most offenders re-jected them out of hand. "I ain't working for no punk ass $5.50 an hour, man," Smoke Dog proclaimed. "That ain't shit." Slim concurred: "Why would I go into a job at $5.15 an hour, $5.25 an hour? Bust my ass from 7:00 in the morning all the way to around 2:00 or 3:00 [in the afternoon]. Why would I do that there when I go out here and it take me about a day and I can knock off about

$600, $700, $800 right there?" Working also meant waiting for a paycheck—intolerable for those accustomed to instant gratification. "Forty [hours] get paid every two weeks, check. You work all that motherfucking time [and then have to wait] for a check[?]" Spanky asked incredulously. As all of us know, the more remote the future reward, the "lower its present value and . . . the less likely [it will] be chosen among current alternatives" (Kirby et al. 1999:78). For street offenders, this was as presupposed as it was a creed to live by.

Jobs severely cramped the offenders' lifestyle as well—requiring them to show up sober and alert, obey authority, and do a pre-specified set of tasks for a defined period of time. Lost freedom and foregone opportunities are unacceptable for those whose lives are premised on "going with the flow" (see also Jacobs 1999a; Wright and Decker 1997). Indeed, legal work represents the "antithesis of the bohemian lifestyle [most offenders prefer to live,] with its strict regime, rules, rigidity, constant surveillance, privations and general authoritarianism" (Gabor et al. 1987:76). For many, the decision *not* to work became rather easy:

> [When I worked,] I was always wanting to go on the streets with my friends, wanting to do things. We gonna go do this or we gonna go over to some gal's house or we got some money set up, we can go rob this nigger for $500, $600. "Damn, I got to go to work." "Come on, let's go rob 'em." Stuff like that. My partners put me up on licks [robberies], big money and I had to go to work. I'm like, well I don't get paid today. They ain't paying me today at work. Take off, go make these licks.—*Ray Ray*

SANCTION THREATS

Rewards—be they financial, pharmacological, or cognitive—are only half of the equation. Crime benefits cannot be considered in the absence of crime risks. And the risks of drug robbery are appealingly small, particularly as they pertain to formal sanction threats. As noted previously, illicit contexts render law unavailable as a matter of course. Participants in black-market enterprise cannot be "victims" and as such, can be exploited with relative impunity. "What he [dealer] gonna do," Slim observed confidently, "call the police and tell [them] I took his drugs from him?" "You can never report a drug-related robbery," Darnell declared. "You [can't] go to the police and say 'he took $1,300 from me in cash and 50 pills [of heroin, worth $500].'" "Come on," J Rock echoed, "get real, fuck that." Even if a police report is made, authorities typically write it off or officiously remark that the victim in question got what he deserved.[3] Bystanders are reticent to intervene and also reluctant to come forward as witnesses; on the streets, the ability to mind one's own business is vital (Jacobs 1999a). Disastrous consequences await those who snitch. Thus, people "see but don't see" (Anderson 1999:133; see also Liska and Warner 1991 on how the fear of crime constrains reporting).

Immunity of this nature does not accompany more ordinary offenses. Not only are structural barriers against reporting absent, there is a much higher risk of third-party intervention. "People can hear you breaking into they car," Lewis revealed, "burglar alarms go off, dogs barking, you see what I'm saying? . . . You got a better chance [with drug robbery], better chance to run off but if you breaking into a car you gonna hear the dog barking, peoples turn the lights on." The threat of official detection is commensurately higher:

> Police come real quick for [burglarizing] people . . . That's how you get caught up . . . walking in people houses. . . . People got alarms, you all know that.—*K-red*

> You rob [burglarize] a house, you caught by the police. You shoplift out of a store, you gonna wind up being caught. —*Snap*

Insulation from official consequences comes at a price, however. Resistance and retribution are part-and-parcel of many offenses, especially those perpetrated against persons who themselves are involved in crime. The threat of victim-retaliation is widely assumed in discussions of drug robbery. Vendors are depicted to be armed, dangerous, and primed to react (see, for example, Bourgois, 1995). Conventional wisdom holds that such persons will not stay in business, or stay in business for long, if they allow themselves to be victimized (Maher and Daly 1996; Johnson et al. 1985). The message that one cannot be trifled with must be communicated with stark clarity (see also Anderson 1999).

It was somewhat surprising to learn, therefore, that "soft" dealers—those disinclined to resist or retaliate—reportedly dominated the street scene. A reflection of drug market circumstances unique to St. Louis or of the particular stereotypes of these respondents, such reports highlight an important perception that guided their actions. "[D]ope dealers out here right now today man," Ray Dog insisted, "[they] are straight up chumps. . . . They are punks. . . . They are the weakest." Do-dirty declared that dope dealers are "the most punk-ass niggers in the world." Ray Ray remarked that he robbed "bitches, bitch-ass fools that ain't gonna do nothing . . . dudes that's weak, that's soft . . . that's real scary that . . . ain't gonna do nothing [and there are a lot of them]."

As a general rule, streetcorner dealers were perceived to be softer than those who sold from houses. They tended to be younger and less likely to be armed—presumably to avoid the double sanction of drug *and* weapons possession (a considerable risk on the open streets). "They don't believe in carrying no guns," Do-dirty reported. "If he get caught he got possession and CCW [carrying a concealed weapon]. So he gonna . . . stash his pistol [away from his body]." Darnell concurred: "Why you have a gun out there? You already gonna catch a dope case, you know what I'm saying? So why catch a concealed weapon [case also]?" Or, as June Bug put it:

> Five out of ten, a drug dealer out there selling drugs ain't got no pistol . . . 'cause he's worried about the police riding on him. See, he can throw the drugs away but it's hard to throw a pistol away 'cause they [police] can go get that pistol.

Though guns could have theoretically been placed somewhere in the surrounding area, they would not be available at the time they were needed most. Off-person hiding also made firearms prone to discovery and theft by covert observers, clearly an undesirable outcome.

In an analysis of Drug Use Forecasting (DUF) data, Decker and Pennell (1995) found that exceedingly small percentages of street-based offenders reported carrying a gun all or most of the time. Firearm possession did tend to be higher among drug sellers, but rates still were quite low. Lizotte et al. (1997), by contrast, found that between one-third and one-half of all juvenile drug sellers reported carrying a gun regularly. It may be the case that, for non-carriers, the threat of arrest outstrips that of being robbed—a testament to more vigorous policing, harsher weapons laws, or simply an underestimation of the real threat of drug robbery. This is, of course, speculative; more research is needed to specify the contingencies that mediate firearm possession within this high-risk group.

Guns aside, we know from the literature that curbside drug dealers typically lack the organizational wherewithal required for even mundane retaliatory action. Their freelance, individual-istic orientation is not conducive to focused payback (see, for example, Decker and Van Winkle, 1996; Jacobs, 1999a). This is especially true for those who deal on high-volume, competitive sets—on which many of our offenders committed their drug robberies. Time spent seeking retaliation can better be spent making money and for many, the opportunity cost of lost sales was too high to justify the effort. "Money, money, they can get that again," Goldie professed. "Ain't got to worry about it. They can make that money back probably in one night." Jay agreed: "What [t]he [victim loses isn't] really no loss to him because of the way he make the money fast. . . . It's a waste of time [to pursue me]." Or as Blackwell observed, "I don't think I'm . . . gonna get retaliated back on by them 'cause they want to go back on they corner and sell drugs. That's what they do, sell drugs."

Indeed, a number of offenders developed a degree of self-assuredness they conspicuously lacked for seemingly less dangerous offenses. Do-dirty, for example (one of the most ruthless members of the sample), claimed he was afraid to shoplift. "I'm scared to steal," he confessed. "I tried it once, you dig? . . . Man,

I got out of the store, they rushed me right over. I can't steal. I'm not no thief." Blackwell made a similar admission. "I wouldn't want to shoplift," he conceded. "[I] never stole nothing a day in my life. . . . I would rather buy what I want out of the store."

With drug robbery, offenders knew what they were getting into. Experience and familiarity engendered a certain sense of confidence. Threats were apparent and prone to being managed. Skills had been honed from repetition. Offending scripts reduced ambiguity (see also Forgas 1979). When outcomes are predictable, sanction risks seem smaller or less ominous than they really are. The fear of the unknown, by contrast, can be too much to handle:

> I used to steal, I used to rob people. I mean just rob people houses, break into houses, take jewelry whatever. I done snatched purses. I done snatched shit off of people's neck you know. . . . That's too risky because you ain't really preparing yourself for something, you're just there and see it and snatch. One day you could snatch the wrong person's shit. 'Cause like I said, when you're in a certain environment you don't know who got a gun with them and who don't. You would be surprised how many people out here on the street, just walking up and down the street looking normal got a gun on them. Some of them not with intent to do crime but intent to protect they self because of where they have to go.—*Jay*

All these factors taken together make drug robbery appear to be the best, most rapid, and most reliable solution to the offenders' pressing material needs (see also Wright and Decker 1997).

MORALISTIC ACTION?

The allure of drug robbery transcended utilitarian notions of risk and reward. A number of offenders waxed philosophical about their motivations, claiming such offenses were activated, at

least in part, by moralistic concerns. The notion of "crime as social control" is nothing new (Black 1983). Since time immemori-
al, people have taken the law into their own hands to right
perceived wrongs. In virtually every society, individuals perceive
"the right to inflict pain or deprivations on others . . . under specified conditions" (Tedeschi and Felson 1994:216). Indeed, vigilantism was once the modal form of conflict resolution; formal
social control arose primarily to limit it.

For some offenders, drug robbery constituted prosocial behavior designed to sanction dealers who had committed some perceived violation. The nature of such violations varied. A number
of offenders couched them in broad terms, alleging that drug robbery represented righteous retribution for the destruction dealers
wrought on persons and entire communities by hawking their evil
wares. The devastating impact of crack, heroin, and other hard
drugs on urban life has been well-chronicled (see, for example,
Bourgois 1995). As self-anointed purveyors of street justice, drug
robbers were going to make dealers pay the consequences. "If
you selling dope [you] messing up the community," Low Down
illustrates, "you know what I'm saying? You gonna have to get
got [robbed] because you [a] person up here killing people."
Loony Ass Nigga agreed: "That dope killing people," he declared, "truly it is. They [dealers] got people looking bad, they
don't feel sorry for nobody, why should I pity them? . . . They ain't
showing no love, I ain't showing none." Drug robbers emerged
as agents on a quasipolitical mission to rectify what they believed
to be a great social wrong:

> Anybody's that selling drugs to us, they killing us. Like I feel
> for the kids, like a mother that's smoking crack and every-
> thing. They stop taking care of they kids because they want
> crack. . . . They send they kids on (inaudible) and everything
> and I look at it like they supposed to take care of they kids
> and everything. When they get they welfare checks and all
> that, they take straight money. They using crack, the ones
> that got kids, they supposed to be eating, they supposed to
> be clothing and all that and them hustlers, they just want
> they money.—*Blackwell*

Some respondents went so far as to claim they were doing *users* a favor (by robbing their suppliers). "If I take it, they can't buy it" was the sentiment typically expressed. A small number had even managed to convince themselves that they were providing a service to their *victims*. "It's better for me to get [them] than it is for the police," Do-dirty illustrates. "See, the police get him, he got to make bond and then he gonna lose out." Three Eyes rationalized similarly: "[I'm doing my victims] a favor. Better me than the police, you know, you get locked up, kept in a cage . . . money gone. . . . I'm just taking your money [but] you still out on the streets." Such intellectualizations are common among those who wish to make harmful conduct seem respectable, and who seek to reduce personal responsibility for it in the process (Bandura 1999:195)

It would be folly, however, to suggest that the offenders were motivated solely by social altruism, or that the altruistic motives they expressed were genuine. In most cases, retributive motives appeared to be grounded in some need to right a perceived *personal* wrong. The nature of such wrongs varied, from blows to self-esteem, to transactional "insults," to affronts to personal dignity. All, however, shared the common theme of an unbalanced state of reciprocity—wherein slighted individuals felt the need to reclaim a perceived loss of social standing. Social psychologists tell us that whenever people find their desired identities impugned, remedial action must be taken to "protect, maintain, and reestablish" them (Tedeschi and Felson 1994:256; Goffman 1971; see also Baumeister and Campbell 1999 on "threatened egotism"). Drug robbery represented a powerful way to do this.

As hard-drug addicts, respondents were especially sensitive about how their status was perceived by others—particularly those who supplied them. Dealers were known to have "big heads," talking down to their customers and treating them in disparaging ways. "Once they start selling drugs they get a big head," Lewis illustrates. "They talk to you like you a kid, you know, and tell you how to spend your money this way and that way." On the streets, this cannot be tolerated; "esteem is so precarious that it can be taken away with just a word" (Anderson 1999:75, 95). Indeed, affronts that casual observers might consider trivial were imbued with profound meaning here. The widespread acceptance of the word "trivial" by middle-class "outsiders" betrays their utter inability "to interpret and make sense of the semiotic significance of opaque social events" (Campbell 1986:122). Seemingly innocuous encounters might very well result in conflicts fraught with reputational—and retributional—meaning:

> When I seen [this dealer] I said, "Hey, what's up Tony, how you doing?" "All right man, just chilling and stuff like that." "Oh man, you looking bad, you still on drugs and stuff like that?" "Yeah, you know." So I kind of take that personal, you know what I'm saying? Why do you look down on me when you probably doing things wrong? . . . I just sit down and think about, OK, so he got all this [money] and then he gonna talk down on me like that? . . . I was like, I'm gonna get this dude.—*Low Down*

> I robbed him 'cause he was talking shit, he pissed me off. Otherwise I just don't do that to people.—*Kilo*

> He didn't know how to talk to peoples . . . like he feel like that [he didn't owe nobody] shit and he could talk to you any kind of way. . . . I didn't like him. . . . We had a few words . . . so I figured that one of these days I would get him.—*Lewis*

Condescension was a sure-fire way for dealers to trigger animosity, particularly given the synergistic relationship they had with their customers:

> These cats [crack dealers] man because they think they better than the next motherfucker, man. . . . Them little cats discriminate the motherfuckers that smoke crack. "Oh he just an old crackhead motherfucker," you see what I'm saying, you know. But what the motherfucker fails to realize is, man, you know, we make you, you don't make us. Without us your crack ain't shit 'cause you will still be stuck with that shit,

you know. So I prefer to get the crack dealers because the majority of them be cats, you know, they don't have no respect for the older dudes, you know. Because, you know, I'm not begging you for anything; I'm buying what I want from you but I still got to be a crackhead motherfucker to you.—*June Bug* (see also Wills 1981 on "downward comparison")

Offenders relished the opportunity to put violators in their proper place, restoring their own status by lowering that of those who impugned them. "When you can get [a] dude [like that], man," Curly beamed, "it's like a trophy. You can say, 'Man, I got that motherfucker, man. I really got him. He's been fucking me over . . . and I got [him],' and it makes you feel good." Baby Doll agreed: "They be looking at us like we really crack fiends, they look down on us so when I got that gun on them, they looking down at this gun. They look how we be looking when we need that crack." June Bug was equally emphatic:

Man, you know this little nigger, (inaudible) this old punk-ass nigger, he called me a motherfucking goddamn crack-head. [Then I] hit him in the head and bust his motherfucking head with a pistol. Get high . . . get high and sit back and think about him. . . . [He was saying,] "motherfucker goddamn it please don't kill me," see what I'm saying? But I'm just another crackhead to his motherfucking ass but he got the nerve to beg for his motherfucking life, you see what I'm saying? So it's fun to me.

For some, taking such action seemed to be almost as reinforcing as the drugs to which they were addicted. "It's like an adrenaline rush," Loony Ass Nigga proclaimed. "Some people go bungee jumping, some people go sky diving, I . . . kick [drug] houses in. . . . It's the same thing, no joke." "I get a kick out of robbing drug dealers," exulted Blackwell. "It's fun . . . real fun . . . it's just something that I really enjoy. . . . It's just like if a crackhead smoke crack and they get that feeling that high, that rush; I feel the same way as a crackhead when they get that pipe when I rob one of these drug dealers out here." Or as Lady Bug put it, "I mean it just give you this supernatural feeling that you can be in control. . . . When I put a gun up to they head I feel good. . . . It make you just be in control and then just to see them frightened, it can give you more energy." "I . . . feel so powerful," Snap remarked. "Just take control. . . . I love that, man . . . that's a [rush]." As the offenders insinuate, such feelings are not limited to robberies committed out of vengeance. However, the satisfaction obtained at these times undoubtedly is sweeter than at any other (see also Feather 1996).

Often, dealer insults were transactional in nature—grounded in conduct specific to some purchase attempt. Lewis, for example, recalled trying to buy $50 worth of heroin for $45—a common tactic on the streets where users try to stretch their money as far as possible. The dealer, however, "took my money and balled it up and threw it in my face, threw it back to me. . . . He wanted to talk to [me] like [I was] a drug addict . . . and I felt he couldn't talk to me that kind of way. . . . I said to myself, 'That's ok . . . I'll be back tonight . . . I'm gonna stalk you.'"

Similar encounters were reported by others:

> Like if you get a rock from them, they tell you you got to pay $50 for one rock. That's an insult . . . A rock isn't nothing but $20. They gonna charge you $50 for a rock?—*J Rock*

> You can go there with your last $20 and they want to give you something real, real small. That will make you mad. He needs to be got [robbed], you know.—*Baby Doll*

Dealers who refused to front drugs or give credit, especially to longtime customers who had proven their brand-loyalty, were perceived to be especially insolent. "Free" drugs typically are requested when users are most desperate, usually after all other means of income-generation have been exhausted. Broke and under pressure to keep the party going, denials can generate nothing short of a full-blown crisis. Violence emerges reflexively to deal with it, aggression ignited by a volatile combination of vengeance and need:

> Like I ask them for something and they don't give it to me. A guy on the street, he selling rock and I told him like this, "Man, look, I'm hurting, I need my motherfucking medicine and I need it right now. . . . I asked for something and you wouldn't give me nothing so now I want it all." . . . He say, "what you talking about?" "I want your motherfucking crack." "I ain't giving you shit." I upped on him, "Give it here," and he give it to me. . . . "You think I'm bullshitting? . . . Give me all your dope and all your money now. . . . You think I'm bullshitting?" I'll rob his ass.—*J Rock*

> I'm down and out and I ain't got nothing coming in . . . and I come to you and you can't do nothing for me. So what the hell am I gonna do? What you think I'm gonna do? I'm gonna rob you, that's all.—*Ray Dog*

> I'm broke and I tried to talk to him about fronting me something . . . so I can get back on my feet . . . he was just in there counting his money and his dope. . . . I done thought about it, man; I could take this. . . . It just came to me, I just went crazy man.—*Smoke Dog*

Being ripped off or shorted was an equally powerful catalyst. When purchasing illicit drugs, every transaction represents an expensive and, to some degree, irretrievable investment. Writing off resources that might have taken significant time and effort to accumulate, often at considerable risk, is not an option; the "sunk costs" are too substantial and generate too much cognitive dissonance (Arkes and Ayton 1999). K-red, for example, reportedly revenge-robbed a dealer of $600 in cash and a gram of heroin (valued at about $250) after being sold just $10 worth of fake heroin. Bacca, trying to collect on a larger drug debt, was told by the debtor that he had "nothing" and to "get out of his face." He promptly went home, loaded his pistol, and returned to rob the seller. Likewise, Jay recounted an incident in which he helped a dealer-associate rehabilitate a house, who tried to "get over" by paying him in crack rather than cash. Drugs are not considered payment in kind, and Jay perceived this to be demeaning of his essential character (by implying that he was a stigmatized "crack-head" whose existence revolved solely around securing the drug). He turned to drug robbery to collect what was perceived to be properly owed to him:

> I do rehabbing on houses . . . and I had did some work on one of his apartments for him, some drywall and stuff and he didn't ever finish giving me all the money 'cause me hanging around, you know, he would give me a little dope here a little dope there to compensate and I told him "I didn't ask you for that shit. . . . I wasn't working for crack, I was working for money," and he felt like he didn't have to give me no money 'cause he had gave me some crack. . . . He owed me $100 at that point. The rest of it he had paid me, but he still owed me $100. I wanted him to give me $100. He didn't want to give me $100 'cause he said he gave me some crack. Then he tried to give me some more crack and I told him I wasn't working for no fucking crack. . . . I said, "I want my money." He said, "I don't owe you no motherfucking money." He said, "Man, I gave you the crack." I said, "Man, I don't work for no fucking crack, man." I said I was working for money. . . . "I want my motherfucking money." He said, "I ain't gonna give you no money, man, 'cause I done gave you too much crack." I turned off like I was gonna walk off. I just went in my [pants] and pulled my gun out. Told him he was gonna give me my money. I took about $400 . . . from him that day.

Perceived insults are one thing; advances against one's very personhood, or "form," as they say on the streets, are quite another. Indeed, threats to one's personal autonomy represented arguably the most serious instance of negative reciprocity. After a drug-market associate snitched to the police on J Rock, he felt irresistibly compelled to take matters into his own hands. "A friend will never tell on nobody," he insisted. "He tell, he rat on me. . . . Three years of my life [in prison] and everything [all the crime] I do I ain't never get caught and that nigger get me caught. . . . That's why I did what I had to do." Lady Bug robbed a dealer for being too sexually forward with her cousin; their relationship was apparently close enough to transform the incident into a personal vendetta that would end only after vengeance. (The subsequent robbery resulted in the shooting of three of the dealer's associates.) Baby Doll fleeced a dealer in retaliation for her own rape a few months prior:

> . . . this guy. He had did something to me, he had raped me. . . . So I had set it in my mind that I had wanted to get him. So I set him up. I told him that somebody wanted to get kind of like an 8 ball or something like that. So . . . I took him on the set to get him robbed.

One may justifiably wonder why respondents turned to robbery as the means to exact revenge. Why not assault or burglarize victims, or deface their property? Why not seek the ultimate payback and kill them? Perhaps drug robbery represents the best combination of financial harm, physical threat, and mental intimidation. Assaults are too simple; black eyes and busted lips heal. Defaced property can be fixed or replaced. Theft without contact is not personal or humiliating enough. Murder generates bodies, and bodies bring heat (something drug robbers dearly want to avoid). Drug robbery mixes the most hurtful elements of property and violent crime, and is perhaps the best way to exact bloodless revenge. Most importantly, offenders can secure exactly what they want—and need—to keep the party going.

Importantly, such revenge need not be directed against the actual person or persons responsible for the activating affront. Imperfect retaliation—drug robberies motivated by the actions of one person but enacted against others—were commonly reported. Respondents often had sold drugs in the past, creating the "necessary and sufficient" conditions for the motive to form. "When somebody robbed me," Do-dirty illustrates, "I robbed another motherfucker. I got mine back. . . . What happen to me I can do it to [some other guy] . . . it's a chain of robbing." Lewis claimed he really wasn't interested in drug robbery until he was robbed himself. "That made me want to start sticking up [others]." Similarly, Darnell used his own victimization experience as motivation to prey on others:

> Yeah. They messed me up pretty bad. So therefore I couldn't regain the clientele that I had on the street before. . . . [No one would] pay me any attention, didn't want to help me out. So that's when the nines [9 mm's] come off the shelf. . . . I'm gonna take it all.

Even those who may have been initially dead-set against stealing the property of others came to realize that turnabout—no matter how indirect—is fair-play. The norm of reciprocity dictates that every action must be met with an equal and opposite reaction. Deficits—be they cognitive, psychological, or material—must be made up as rapidly as possible. This is especially important in street culture, where inaction symbolizes weakness, and weakness signals vulnerability. (See Takahashi 2000 on the principle of "generalized exchange.")

DISCUSSION

From no other work category, licit or illicit, can one earn the sums offered by drug robbery with so little effort. Even tiny rewards can look large when earned in such fashion, and the bounties seized here are seldom tiny. Moreover, they come in the precise form offenders desire, permitting party pursuits to continue uninterrupted. Formal sanction risks are perceptibly small and informal ones (i.e., victim retaliation) are manageable. This makes anticipated rewards that much more attractive. Such offenses also take but seconds to complete, which makes the risk "quick" and seem smaller / less threatening than it really is (Felson 1987).

Material deficits are relieved, but only fleetingly, since money and drugs typically are burned as fast as they are obtained. Offenders thereby create the conditions that drive them to their next crime (see Wright and Decker 1997). To the degree that drug robbery promises a reliable solution to their problems, the cycle of deficit to surplus and back to deficit will become ceaselessly intense. A no-holds-barred mentality may be cultivated in which offenders believe they can drug themselves into oblivion and never be without. Robberies, like the drug use that inspires them, may well become habitual (see also Gabor et al. 1987; McSweeney and Swindell 1999).

Seemingly irrational to outsiders, such behavior makes perfect sense in the circumscribed world of the streets. Here, status is a function of the totality with which one can slough off the mundane concerns that plague others and embrace instead a life shot through with action (see Katz 1991:297). Burning money is functional, the "cost of raising or maintaining one's status" (Wright and Decker 1994:45). Coolness is king. To be cool, one must do what one wants to do, when one wants to do it. Coolness means maintaining control over one's own destiny and refusing "to allow others to determine or influence one's life" (Campbell 1986:120). Coolness means showing contempt for everything that conventional society deems correct and appropriate (Fleisher 1998:138). Coolness "means remaining a free spirit in a world which persistently seeks to tame" and crush that spirit (Campbell 1986:120). To live conventionally is to live the life of the square—a life of rationality and restraint, sublimation and self-control, boredom and repetition. It is a life of false consciousness and failed self-actualization, a life these offenders want no part of.

The looking glass of the streets is especially strong, and its glare is felt by those who can't measure up with sustained intensity. Indeed, those unable to keep the action going face an immediate threat to their social standing (Wright and Decker 1994:201). They must not only stare failure full in the face, but suffer social devaluation in a world where legitimate means of status attainment have largely ceased to exist.

The psychic benefits of drug robbery should not be underestimated either. Recall that the lives of these offenders are very much spinning out of control. Desperation shadows them like a pulp fiction detective. Uncertainty is the only constant. In the moment of the offense, the world stands still. Offenders enjoy a momentary opportunity to impose order on chaos. They can exert control in a bubble of self-contained action, locking into the brute being that lies at the core of their self (see also Adler 1985). They can revel in the serenity of dominance, testing and displaying primal capacities that cannot be tested or displayed elsewhere (cf. Heimer 1988). They can embrace fatality to "manifest transcendent powers of control" (Katz 1988:220). For those whose self-worth is so existentially grounded, such an experience may be matched by few others.

It would be unwise to overemphasize the self-help or "secret social control" function of drug robbery (see also Peterson 1999). The offense is committed first and foremost for material gain. Offenders want drugs and cash, they want as much of them as they can get, and they want them *now.* Compliance—not harm—is the goal; violence is incidental, often disfavored, and tends to happen only if "forced" by the victim (Reidel 1993:159; see also Felson and Messner 1996). This is not to suggest that depriving victims of property is not harming them but rather, that the harm is not *truly* injurious. Vengeance-crimes, by contrast, are predicated on angry—rather than instrumental—aggression, assault not predation (Felson and Messner 1996; but see Black 1983). Revenge is tangential to drug robbery, important, but an added bonus.

Talk of drug robbery as moralistic action may therefore be just that. Techniques of neutralization are commonly used by deviants to make bad deeds look more honorable than they really are (Sykes and Matza 1957). As Mills (1940) reminds us, the reasons people give for their actions are not themselves without reasons. This is particularly true when offenders can convince themselves that their reputation is at stake, or when audiences are middle-class researchers whom offenders may perceive to be passing judgment. In such instances, harmful conduct is invested with "high moral purpose," which not only "eliminates self-censure but . . . engages self-approval in the service of destructive exploits. What was once morally condemnable becomes a source of self-valuation" (Bandura 1999:196).

Yet how "condemnable" a deed is drug robbery? More to the point, how "good" can such a bad deed be? In the culture of the badass, few offenses communicate a more powerful message about one's essential character. The streets are a stage. They are a place where dignity, honor, and respect are won and lost on a daily basis. Talking about how tough, poised, or resourceful one might be is not enough. One must prove it through action. Jamming a gun in someone's face and seizing their valuables does this in the most emphatic way possible. Doing so against another criminal puts the perpetrator on a whole different level. Reputation is currency, and the resultant riches can match the material ones the offense promises. As Macleod (1987:26) insists:

> To be "bad" is literally to be good. . . . [It] is inextricably bound up with the premium put on masculinity, physical toughness, and street wisdom. . . . To be bad is the main criterion for status [on the streets]; its primacy cannot be overemphasized.

In the final analysis, it is not just a question of keeping the party going but how one is able to do it. Readers must keep in mind that motivation is an embedded construct operating in the foreground of offenders' lives. To ignore this is to ignore the larger phenomenological context in which all decisions to offend are activated (see also Groves and Lynch, 1990; Katz, 1988). The victims in this case just happen to be "tarnished" people (Shover 1975), who sell outlawed goods, and who may or may not have behaved in disrespectful ways. Those intent on robbing them couldn't ask for a better justification.

NOTES

1. Such claims take on special resonance in the present era, one in which record numbers of Americans are forsaking currency for the convenience and safety of plastic. This "revolution" in cash-avoidance

behavior amassed nearly $1 trillion of credit debt in 1999 alone (CBS News 2000; see also Felson 1997).

2. This is not to say that respondents will fail to exercise versality when the occasion calls for it. Rather, it is to suggest that drug robbery is the preferred crime, one they report turning to first.

3. Apparently, some dealers actually call the authorities, under the pretext that their "insurance money" or "job check" had been stolen. Police typically reject such claims as bogus.

CHAPTER THREE

Target Selection

T HE STUDY OF target selection is part and parcel of a more generalized concern with the chemistry of crime—the factors necessary and sufficient for any offense to occur (Felson 1987). Interacting dynamically with motivation, suitable targets shape the opportunity structure for, and trajectory of, criminal events in discrete contexts. Obviously, the best *drug robbery* targets are the most visible, valuable, accessible, and perceptibly easiest to take. This makes perfect sense. Drug robbers are utilitarians. They want to score as much as they can as quickly as possible, and to encounter minimum resistance in the process. The harder the target and the less it is worth, the lower its marginal utility. The harder the target and the more time required to "take it," the greater the risk of intervention, both formal and informal.

Insofar as drug robbers are rational decision makers, the selection process will be a prudent one. Contingencies will be appraised, costs and benefits evaluated, and outcome probabilities assigned particular weights. Only after a thoroughgoing assessment will the optimal course of action be revealed, and acted upon.

Most drug robbers, however, are not nearly so calculating. They maintain a rationality that is limited at best (Bennett and

Wright 1984). Immediate needs, blunted judgment, and pressing information-processing demands mandate that decisions be made rapidly, often on the basis of limited data. This creates a dilemma, as drug robbers confront "two seemingly conflicting demands, one calling for action, the other counseling [deliberation]" (Wright and Decker 1994:62). The present chapter explores this dynamic tension, and how it shapes the form and content of drug robbers' decisions.[1]

THE PROCESS

At the most basic level, target-selection is about operating when settings are most likely to be victim-rich. The greater the dealer density, the wider the range of options from which drug robbers could pick. The more options, the better their chance of choosing the most lucrative target (see also Pirolli and Card 1999). High-density sets also provide the opportunity to pick the "softest" victim, one whose retaliatory potential is perceived to be especially poor relative to expected rewards. Extravagant heists, after all, can be enjoyed to their fullest only if they are seized without suffering grave injury or death.

Dealer density hinges on a multiplicity factors, but consumer demand is principally implicated. Demand, in turn, largely is a function of time. Like other street crime, the vast majority of drug sales occur after nightfall. "Usually dark hours is when [dealers] . . . are out," Jay explained. "They ain't gonna be out too much like a time like this [early afternoon]. . . . Most dealers sleep in the daytime. They be working all night. . . . Anywhere from 8 at night to 6 or 7 in the morning." Friday- and weekend-nights were especially busy. Due largely to employment periodicities, customers' discretionary time and disposable income tend to be higher during these periods than at any other. Drug income comes fast and furiously, and sellers cannot afford to forego promised windfalls. Greater drug and cash reserves are needed to service this demand, increasing the number and attractiveness of would-be targets. "[It's] fat . . . on Friday nights," Buck proclaimed. "Most of the time dope dealers carry a lot of dope on Fridays, they sell a lot on Fridays."

On or near the first of the month was perhaps the best time for drug robbers to troll. This period marked the disbursement of public transfer payments—Social Security, Aid to Families with Dependent Children (AFDC), and disability checks. Such payments were in the several-hundred dollar range, and sellers reportedly could expect to pocket a significant portion from customers who received them. "The beginning of the month . . . that's when the most money out," Loony Ass Nigga observed. "Everybody get they check, social security checks come out. . . . That's a couple of G's (thousands of dollars) right there. . . . I'm talking about these people have big time money [and they spend it on drugs]." J Rock concurred: "The first of the month where the money at," he insisted. "That's where the money at. . . . The bills [checks] be out, boom, boom, got all that shit out there. . . . [I'll be out there too]." As Bourgois et al. (1997:162–63) point out, the illicit economy is facilitated and energized by the very institutions of government that seek to suppress drug use. Though recent welfare reform legislation is intended to address this problem (by reducing the amount of public transfer money and changing its form so as to make it less liquid; Jacobs 1999a:47), the effects have apparently not been felt on the streets. Drug robbers responded accordingly.

It stands to reason, however, that targeting drug sellers during their most active periods may bring undue risk. Police enforcement typically peaks with transactional activity; the more active the drug market, the more intensely it tends to be interdicted. Though drug robbery is attractive because it lacks official sanction threats, police can stumble on such offenses just as easily as any other enacted on the open street. The net of social control is wide and democratic, imperiling all who do wrong. Armed and skulking the streets, drug robbers faced very real consequences in the event they were "flagged" by a passing cop:

> . . . carry a gun . . . get flagged with a gun, look what you got now. You got a CCW. State gonna drop it, Feds gonna pick it up then you go in the Federal joint.—*Slim*

Owing to pressing needs, the vast majority of respondents did not appear to be fazed. Quite the contrary; the "hotter" the corner, the more attractive, paradoxically, it seemed to become. Vendors subject to constant police scrutiny were wholly unlikely to be armed, even less so than normal. This created the perfect victim, one flush with cash and/or drugs yet defenseless. "Most corners that I [target] dudes on," Curly reasoned, "are called hot spots.... [Dealers] can't stand on this corner ... with no gun, man, because the police might pull over any time and make everybody get against the wall and I'm just saying that stuff's common ... " Do-dirty agreed:

> Because when the police riding around it's enough they out there selling drugs on the street. So if the police ride down here, you know what I'm saying, they got a pistol and it's ... sticking out. Well then they going to jail for dealing drugs and a CCW. And you don't know if these police gonna shoot you if you just try to take your gun out and lay it on the ground. They might shoot you. They think you trying to shoot them. So I catch the street dealers.

Precise information was needed to identify exactly which of the many potential targets justified specific attention. Failure to prequalify victims risks selecting someone who either is not worth one's while, or who presents too grave a threat relative to the expected bounty (see also Lejeune 1977). Why chance injury or death to secure an unknown and perhaps meager take? As Kilo declared, "If you gonna do it, you might as well go for the big money, a large sum.... You got to make it worth while." (On balancing risk and reward in robbery, see Cook 1976.)

With these criteria in mind, it was not surprising to learn that house dealers were the preferred quarry. Dedicated locations provide protection from police scrutiny and a place to get high. This attracts substantial business, often repeated over a short period of time. Cash is made hand over fist, so sizable drug reserves must be maintained to meet consumer demand. "I only go to dope dealer houses," Three Eyes insisted, "the ones that got money ... $30,000 or $40,000.... You can't get much ... on the streets." Spanky recognized that he "could . . . just [rob] a cat around the corner or something but I know they probably wouldn't have had nothing but maybe $1,000 theyself. They [don't] have no money." Others made similar declarations:

> The big boys is the best boys because those boys you never can tell, you might go their house and get $20,000 or $30,000 out of there, you dig? You might go in there and get $150,000 'cause they be having safes in they houses. You might go in there and get like 30 or 40 keys [kilos] out of there.—*Ray Dog*

> Forget them . . . little dope dealers. I like the big dope dealers, the ones that got the money, cars, Lexus and all that, Volvos and stuff like that. They the ones with the money. . . . Them the ones with the scroll [cash].—*Smoke Dog*

Some came to this realization over time, graduating to house robberies after realizing that curbside vendors could not offer "real money:"

> I don't do no petty [drug] robberies like I used to, you know, when I was little, well not little, but you know, a few years ago. I would just do petty robberies, $10 or $20 for nothing. But now, it's like I got to get me a couple of G's. I want some grand before I, you know, that's worth it, you know what I'm saying. Kick in, get you a couple of G's, but a couple of hundred, I wouldn't do it for a couple of hundred when I do it. If it ain't over $1,000 I ain't messing with it.—*Loony Ass Nigga*

The paradox is that large rewards come at high risk. House sellers lack the "softness" of their curbside counterparts. Most are heavily armed and unafraid to use deadly force. Observers often are present, increasing the likelihood of resistance (in part, due to its greater reputational importance; see Felson 1982). Approaching predators can be more easily spotted and intercepted. Even if entry is successful, offenders will be hard-pressed to know what they will face beyond the door. Multiple parties must be rapidly accounted for and subdued. Unfamiliar environs render outcomes less predictable. Chaos clouds judgment, leading to mistakes with possibly fatal consequences.

For Blackwell, the perceived lack of control was too much to handle. "I would have a problem robbing [one]," he confessed. "You go busting in somebody house or you go up to somebody door talking about it's a robbery, shit . . . you better believe he gonna have his gun setting right here beside him . . . your ass gonna get blasted then. . . . So I figure I catch the street dealer. . . . See, you already know the street dealers ain't got no pistol on them." Shot during a previous house robbery attempt, J Rock simply didn't "trust that . . . shit no more"—implying a preference for less fearsome, though less lucrative, streetcorner prey.

Many echoed similar sentiments, but recognized that the comparatively inferior take offered by street dealers required specific measures to ensure that those selected indeed were worth it. A number of methods were devised to obtain such proof. One involved a rather direct tactic of approaching prospective victims under the guise of wanting to make a purchase. Admittedly bold, such a strategy is not as risky as it sounds. Many curbside drug sales are initiated precisely in this fashion, and vendors must be amenable lest they sacrifice precious business, especially on competitive sets. Feigning interest, drug robbers would determine whether or not proposed victims were viable:

> Talk to 'em. "Like, what's you copping?" [he'll say]. Like, I'll probably say . . . "I can get an ounce of cocaine," but I ain't got the money for an ounce, and he say, "Well, I got [ounces]." Bam, you just told on yourself that you deal in ounces of cocaine. I'm gonna get you, like that.—*Crazy Jack*

> I'll get close to 'em [by making drug buys] just to see what type of person they are, what quality of drugs they have, how much money, how much drugs they have.—*Bacca*

Physical ploys were also effective in bringing this information to the surface, ploys "widely appreciated by street robbers as [a use-

ful way to] show where and how much . . . victim[s are] carrying"
(Katz 1988:174):

> Like if I go with a $100 bill, then if he come out with all this
> money in his pocket, then he got a bag full of heroin, a bag
> full of rocks. Then I'll say, "O.K., that's my pick." He set his
> self up to be robbed.—*Lewis*

> I showed him a $10 bill and maybe 15 ones under the bottom
> [to him, it looked like a lot of cash]. I wanted to let him know
> I wanted to get a gram [of heroin, about $200]. . . . The roll
> looked nice and big like I had a couple hundred bucks
> there. . . . He pulled [this] whole roll of money out of his
> pocket [and that's when I knew he was a good guy to select].
> —*Blackwell*

In most cases, however, offenders needed some way to justify their
initial presence. Manufacturing affiliation artifically through a
"cold buy" is possible, but not always easy; lacking social history, buyers might well be perceived to have ulterior motives, and
be rejected outright. Though cold buys generally will succeed
among more indiscreet / desperate traffickers, their usefulness for
prudent vendors is questionable. And prudent vendors are precisely the ones drug robbers want most to target: desperate sellers tend to be poor, and poor sellers tend not to make good
victims. "You can't go up to the person and say 'Let me cop from
you,'" YoYo explained, "because that person does not know you
and therefore they be like, you might be five-0 [police] or whatever, you know." "The person that don't know you," Ray Dog
continued, "see you coming and burn out real quick. . . . The person that know gonna sit there, gonna wait on you because he
know you." Slim agreed. "You got to make yourself known first,"
he insisted, "you got to let people know who you is because . . .
ain't no way you gonna let me [get close to you otherwise]."

Being introduced by a middleman represented an effective solution to this problem. Network researchers tell us that transitivity is a hallmark of tie-generation, regardless of social context:

Person A knows person B, person B knows person C, person B introduces person A to C. In drug markets, transitivity is particularly crucial: Multiple weak ties generate contacts that lead to an expansive web of potential targets. The more connected one is, the richer one's opportunity structure (cf. Granovetter 1973):

> How do I find dealers to target? Through someone else, someone that knows that person.... Like, if me and you friends, you know people that I don't know and I know people that you don't know, but me and you are close [so we find out targets from each other].—*Bacca*
>
> ... if you don't know them, they ain't gonna deal with you, no way. You got to know somebody that know them real personally, 'cause if you can't call their name they won't fuck with you. This guy knew him [and that was my point of entry].—*Jay*
>
> [You] have to get with the person that knows that person in order to get with you all. So once you get introduced to that person and everything seems to be ok, then that person start dealing with you they self. ... I just couldn't go and do it myself, I had to have someone to do it for me, and then once we got to know one another, then I can go and do it myself. —*YoYo*

FAMILIAR TARGETS?

Such comments imply that the easiest dealers to target are those with whom one already is familiar—a person one knows and associates with. Why wait for introductions, a significant hassle for those with pressing needs, when easier prey is available and ready to exploit? Routine activity patterns imply overlapping networks and modes of activity. Run-ins are frequent, search time minimal. Defensibility and reward information tend to be known as a matter of course. There also is an intuitive understanding of how such persons are likely to react during the offense. Contingencies can be identified with greater precision, increasing the likely success of the crime. Not surprisingly, the vast majority of victims of predatory crimes (drug robberies noth-withstanding) involve perpetrators and targets who know one another, often intimately (see, for example, Wolfgang 1958).

Yet most drug robbers insisted that targeting those one knows was foolhardy. Acquaintanceships increased the odds of recogni-tion and hence, retribution. At first glance, this would seem to contradict their earlier claims, but only if readers fail to grasp the distinction between *knowing* someone and *knowing of* them. On the streets, to "know of" denotes a kind of superficial familiarity, a tie that is weak but one which involves mutual awareness and reciprocal recognition. To "know someone," by contrast, is to know them in the true sense of the word. The tie involves signif-icant reciprocality, shared social history, and experiential knowl-edge. Targeting someone one *knows of* need not, and usually did not, result in retribution—particularly in light of specific mea-sures designed by drug robbers to thwart that possibility (see Chapter 5). This was not the case with the latter. "You rob some-body you *know* [my emphasis]," Crazy Jack explained, "they might kill you. They know where you at, they know where you hanging at." No matter how easy or substantial the score, the greater perceived certainty of consequences simply was not worth it (but see Katz 1988:174–75):

> I ain't gonna rob nobody [I know]. If I rob [him], I'm pretty sure [he] would know my voice. . . . If I be growing up with you all your life and I robbed you, I would be on the run. . . . [You gonna be knowing me] since we was like this [younger]. . . . If I rob [an associate] I'll have to kill him 'cause he will know me and he'll be looking for me. . . . Then I be-ing having to watch my back. . . . I'm not gonna come back and make like it never happened.

Three Eyes and Slim agreed, respectively:

> Like, say, for instance, you are my friend. You are a drug deal-er and I want to rob you but we been knowing each other

about two or three years so I can't personally do it. If I do it
I would actually have to kill you, see what I'm saying? . . . Because he know me.

If he's a regular and he stay on that block or whatever, then
in that area it's a taboo. . . . But if it's a new guy on the block
and you ain't never seen him and you want to know who he
is and he trying to get a fresh start out here, go on and get
him. . . . Someone strange, I got to have him. . . . I don't rob
my friends, I do not do that. That's where that taboo comes
in at. You don't rob your friends. Someone strange, I got to
have him.

Ray Dog insisted that the whole idea of robbing a friend was
ridiculous, not because it violated basic loyalties—which are surprisingly weak (by middle-class standards) to begin with—but
because of its sheer impracticality. Identification was all but certain, even if one were to don a disguise (a common practice during the enactment phase). "I rob strangers better," he proclaimed,
"because they don't know me. See friends know me, they know
your voice, they know how you walk, how you talk, they know
everything. . . . [Even with a ski mask,] you can't . . . go up there
tell him, 'Look nigger, up it.' 'Oh man, Ray, that you, man,' you
know."

This is not to suggest that known dealers were never targeted.
Desperation could drive even the most reluctant of offenders to
rob his friends. "If push came to shove, yeah, I probably would
rob my best friend if I needed to during those times," Darnell confessed. Curly claimed he would grant an acquaintance the opportunity to "gift" him some dope first. "I give you an option,
man," he explained. "I ask you to give me some of that dope and
I won't take all of it. . . . If he hesitate, [I'll take it all]." More often
than not, however, drug robbers would resolve the dilemma by
enlisting an accomplice unknown to the mark to commit the robbery in their place. Having accurate information of the target's
movements, defensibility, support, and goods, the contracting offender would relay the intelligence to their "hit men," who then
performed the job (see also Reidel 1993:151 on "leaksmen"):

> If I know this person and he know me I set him up, have somebody else to rob him so he might, oh well, this nigger right here robbed me and I know where he live. I'll just have him set up, have somebody else to rob him and the person that robbed him, we just split it 'cause I put him on the lick and plus it was my lick so we'll just split it.—*Ray Ray*

Low Down and Blackwell recall situations in which they played this role for a friend:

> I have a couple of friends that, like, "OK, I know this dude over here, he got this right here." I went to school with this [one] guy. We pretty cool. He was like, "I know this dude name of Anthony [pseudonym] you know, he making all paper [lots of money]." He, like, "Yeah, and he hustles too." . . . So what happened, the guy [Anthony] don't know me but my friend know me. So what happened, he [my friend] said, "Hey, man, [he's got a] half an ounce." That's cocaine, that's like $500 worth of cocaine. . . . See, [you] could make at least about $1,200 if you rock it up. So I went over to rob him, you know, he [my friend] set it up.—*Low Down*

> "I know where a sweet robbery at," he [friend] said, "very sweet." I say, "What's the price?" He say, "he got $4,000 and some [more] in his pocket. He been making it all morning." [Asked why this friend called Blackwell and not someone else, Blackwell replied that this has happened before, where he] jumped down on crack dealers and dope [heroin] dealers right on the spot.—*Blackwell*

Though such ventures took time and effort, the benefits outweighed the costs: Inside information produced a guaranteed, often considerable take that the two offenders could split—entirely acceptable in relationships built on "symbiotic greed" (DEA 1997). Meanwhile, the proxy who committed the offense ensured continued anonymity for the offender who organized the scheme. Even if consequences were to befall the former, it wasn't the organizer's prerogative to worry about it. As Jay observed, "It might come back at him, that's on him. He got to take care of his self. I got to take care of myself, you know."

There were important lessons to learn from those who failed to take familiarity into account. Low Down witnessed the brutal demise of a partner who had robbed one familiar dealer too many. He ultimately was killed after two prior retaliation attempts. "I stayed away from him," Low Down recalled. "I could have been riding with him and they [enemies] seen me and thought I had something to do with it." Robbing a stranger-dealer more than once was misguided in a similar sense; anonymity could no longer be maintained or taken for granted. "You never go back and strike the same [victim]," Do-dirty warned. "Never do that. . . . [Y]ou rob a person one time then you go back a second time and try to rob them, they gonna be recognizing you." This, according to Lewis, would most assuredly result in a "gun-down."[2]

Familiarity, or the lack thereof, was important in a geographic sense as well. The majority of offenders refused to prey on victims in or around the neighborhood where they spent most of their time. To do so risked certain exposure (see also Feeney 1986:62; for an opposing view, see Brantingham and Brantingham 1981). As Slim asked, "Why would I rob somebody where I rest my head [sleep] at? Why would I bring heat where I rest my head at, where I stay at? That don't make sense." YoYo concurred: "If I gonna do some dirt I don't want [nobody] to know where I stay." Baby Doll put these sentiments into perspective:

> They [victims] know where you stay at, know where you hang out. . . . [Doing a drug robbery in your "home neighborhood"] that's like putting your life on the line, you know what I'm saying? They can go on up and kill you. . . . I try to have a safe place to live, lay my head. When I go home I know I'm safe there, I ain't got to worry about nobody kicking my door in or chasing me, chasing me down, something like that, you know.

Drug robbers plotted their activities accordingly. Buck, for example, limited his offenses to East St. Louis, Illinois, several miles from his north St. Louis, Missouri, neighborhood and separated by the Mississippi River. "It's easier for me to commit a robbery over there than come into St. Louis. . . . They don't know me that well [over there]. . . . I won't have that much of a chance of them walking up on me in the street." Slim, likewise, restricted his offenses to St. Louis City, staying in objectively close but perceptually distant St. Louis County (the two are geographically separate entities). "If I come out of this county and go down there and do my dirt down there I ain't bringing no dirt out here. Plus nobody don't know where I staying out here." Smoke Dog did the same, committing his robberies in the city and retiring to the safety of his "granny's" house in the county afterward:

> [P]eople riding around in the city looking for me, I'm out here chilling, . . . They ain't gonna find me. . . . You won't find that house unless I bring you to it and show you how to get there. We got so many ways to get to my house, we cool; you ain't gonna find it no type of way unless I show you. . . . You wouldn't believe, some of the guys down there [in the city], they don't even know where [the county] is, man; they never even been out of the projects, man, for real.

The bottom line is that the offenders realized the importance of not "working" where they slept. Using one or more safe zones as a base of operation, they sought to establish separation between grounds intended for "hunting" and those geared toward habitation. As Brantingham and Brantingham (1981:37) note, areas that may be *objectively* available to would-be offenders may, at the same time, be *perceptually* off-limits. Merry (1981) conceptualizes this through the notion of cognitive mapping, "subjective representations imposed on the physical realities of space" that assess the relative safety of some geographically mediated course of action (see also Wright and Decker 1994:87–88). By choosing distal venues, drug robbers generated an added layer of protection: Even if their anonymity somehow was blown, the likelihood of victims finding them remained small.

SURVEYING TARGETS

Given the microstructural and geographic constraints under which the drug robbers operated, the importance of surveillance and focused observation becomes self-evident. Targets needed to be cultivated on an ongoing basis to have any hope of consistent success. Every day could be meaningful, but only with effort. Attentiveness might yield an immediate victim or one to be exploited later. Having a repository of future victims was essential for generating steady income—especially important when times got tough. Pirolli and Card's (1999:670) analogy of the web-building spider is instructive here, organisms who are able to process (eat) one insect while "queuing up" others (in the web) to eat later. In uncertain environments, such tactics are critical to survival.

Surveillance is understandably fretful for impulsive offenders with pressing needs, but it need not be difficult or time-consuming. The neighborhoods within which drug robbers operated were saturated with activity. Though not always blatant, sellers could be observed easily—particularly during the target-rich times in which drug robbers preferred to operate. Prowling through alleys or lurking behind foliage, substantial information could be secured rapidly, at relatively low risk. Information pertaining to defensibility, activity patterns, and natural surveillance was especially sought-after:

> Just observe everything . . . because I just see the type of [behaviors] he have, see if he poking [for a gun] anywhere in the front or in the back [of his pants] anywhere, see how many times he go in the little gangway where he go get his drugs. See when his friends ain't being around him.—*Blackwell*

> I stalk my vantage point late at night, I pick the peoples that I want to rob, you know, and I observe them and I watch them. . . . Watch him go home at night, watch him where he stay at, watch him where he comes, the dudes [he hang with]. Sit back in the alleys, sit back in the bushes or in the gangway, you know, getting ready to make my move . . . do what I have to do.—*Lewis*

Expected rewards, however, tended to be foremost in the offenders' minds, so all else being equal, the "right mark" typically was the busiest. Income is directly correlated with sales activity, so the more active the seller, the more bounty for the taking. Do-dirty claimed this to be a characteristic of solitary vendors, at least among those operating on the streets. (See Jacobs and Potenza 1991 on the "representativeness heuristic.")

> You choose . . . the one that always do it alone. . . . That's the one have all the money and all the dope, the loner. . . . You choose the niggers, ones that you find, you know, you always finding the scariest one, the one that always do it alone. . . . That's the one have all the money and all the dope, the loner. . . . Because the loner is the people that, his stones is bigger than the rest of the [peoples'] stones. He got . . . people that come to him . . . then look at his pockets. His pockets be standing out like this here. He normally folds his money up and just sticks it in his pocket. He never put it all together. He always just ball it up and throw it in his pocket. Then he goes to count his money and he usually puts it in his mouth. That is when you know his pockets full. And if he been out there all day long he gonna make between $1,500 and $2,000.—*Do-dirty*

As much as offenders would like it to be otherwise, past experience is not a guarantee of future outcomes. The stakes simply are too high to forego scrutiny, so typifications needed to be confirmed. "I [gotta] . . . peep them out first," Lil' Player insisted. "I got to know what they got." Darnell would "sit back and analyze. . . . I know if he running like that, like, he done a lot of business. . . . You have to observe, be smart about it." As Slim put it, "I watches my peoples. I sit back and observe for awhile . . . see how he getting it and how long he sell it. . . . [If] he's trying to get that last dollar on the streets, I'll be at him." The importance of, and patience for, focused observation rises in direct proportion to the perceived magnitude of the expected score:

> It may take a week, it may take only two days, you know, but
> ... if you really want 'em you gonna watch 'em. If you got to
> stake out all night you will do that 'cause you, like, damn,
> that's a lot of money. That's a lot of paper. You plot on it.
> —*Loony Ass Nigga*

The best of targets might be hidden in plain sight, so attention to
detail was critical. Bacca, for instance, came to learn that a small
grocery store was actually a front for a large dealing operation.
Such fronts are commonplace in street drug markets; illicit transactions are integrated into licit contexts, thereby camouflaging
the fact that illegal behavior is indeed going on (see Hamid 1998).
Sifting through past observations, Bacca put "two and two together" to identify a virtual treasure trove of riches (see also Pirolli and Card 1999:646 on information filtering):

> You could see the big drug dealers, they drive in, go around
> the back and they'll come, they'll be in for a minute, they'll
> leave. . . . I have a cousin that lives on the north side that was
> also going over there. I used to see him going over there but
> when I see his car I used to think he was just going to the store
> but I just thinking, why was he going around the back? And
> I know he's a big drug dealer and everybody saying this
> Arab's [store owner] a big drug dealer. . . . Now he sells
> drugs to big drug dealers and he was keeping his drugs, his
> dope in the store. He had powder, he had marijuana, he had
> everything, I mean everything.

OPPORTUNISTIC ROBBERIES

All of this implies an invariably rational orientation to the selection process, in which offenders observe, assess, survey, and
stalk their prey, and act only after extensive prequalification.
Most assuredly, this was *not* the case. The frequency with which
drug robbers simply "ran into" prospective victims should not be
discounted. At times, targets seemed to materialize almost mag-

ically—crossing paths with respondents at the right (or wrong, depending on one's viewpoint) place and time. Such encounters should not be surprising. Street life is fluid. Relations are "open-ended and interlocking" (Katz 1991:297), creating a "powerful tendency to bring offenders face to face" (Wright and Decker 1997:62). Isomorphic lifestyles enhance conditions that lead to run-ins. The public arena in which drug sellers operate makes them vulnerable as a matter of course.

Opportunistic robberies are "spur-of-the-moment" affairs that involve little in the way of advance planning or "casing" of targets (Katz 1991:286; see also Dietz 1983; Feeney 1986). The offender "sees a vulnerable target from which to gain some immediate reward, and does not preplan considerations of attack." (Pettiway 1982:263). Target selection and enactment are merged into one continuous process. Motivation, in the "pure" sense of the term, need not be present; serendipity provides all the motivation necessary—given the drug robbers' insatiable thirst for cash and drugs.

"I wasn't even thinking about robbing nobody," Smoke Dog illustrates—recalling an incident where he chanced upon a crack dealer waiting on line at Popeye's Chicken. "No, I'm cool for real. I wasn't thinking trying to take nobody's stuff." When the would-be mark broached the idea of a sale (to occur later, at the dealer's residence), Smoke Dog's mind quickly changed:

> I'm thinking to myself, why should I buy this and he a punk anyway, I'll just take it. So I took it from him. Give me all this, I want everything. And he gave me all the dope [about 5 oz. worth of crack, valued at about $5,000 wholesale]. I smacked him in the face with it. You know, when you hit somebody too hard and like bust they head, you know they gonna grab they face, so he grabbed his face and he just laid on the ground. I guess he thought I was gonna go on and kill him or whatever but I walked on out of the house.

Driving around, Blackwell likewise happened on an opportunity too good to pass up. "One of these young guys come up to my car asking me if I wanted to buy some drugs," he explained. "So I told him yes, I would like to buy some drugs . . . got out of the car and I took my pistol and just put it up against his head." V-O described a similar encounter:

> Yeah, me and my brother, we was just riding in his car and stuff and we were riding around and then this dude, he walked up to my brother. . . . We just out riding and then we stopped at a red light and he walked upon us talking about did you want to buy something. . . . He was about to sell [my brother some weed] and my brother just got out of the car and put the gun on him [and we robbed him].

YoYo unexpectedly came across a mark on a random visit to an associate's house. "Didn't even know the dude," she spoke of the individual she ultimately beat up and robbed. "Only thing we knew was he had [cashed] a paycheck, he was smoking dope and we was gonna [take both]." Likewise, J Rock ambled down the street one evening, only to find two persons in a parked car packaging a substantial amount of marijuana. Target selection became a "no-brainer":

> I just walking down the street one night . . . and I seen two boys that they was in the car with weed, all weed and I looked and I looked. I know that's for me, yeah, it's right there in my face. . . . I seen them on the car there bagging the weed up. They had about two pounds of weed and money . . . and everything. . . . I . . . g[o]t the shit.

For Do-dirty, choosing targets was a simple matter of trolling until the right one fell into his lap—opportunism with an added measure of intent:

> I cruise around neighborhoods mostly every day like that to find out where the dope dealers are [to rob], you know. . . . I

> left out of JVL. I'm coming up from Dr. Luther King going to-
> ward Kingshighway. I make a left on Kingshighway. See, first
> I started in JVL looking. Couldn't find nobody in JVL so I go
> over on Evans. See, I know these little cats on Evans, they
> usually be out. I didn't see them. So I say, O.K., it was about
> 12:00 [midnight]. I'm gonna find somebody, you know. I go
> up on Kingshighway and Page that dude standing out flag-
> ging, you know.—*Do-dirty*

Capitalizing on serendipity meant attending to dramaturgical
cues as well. Drug sellers are widely known to present a public
persona at odds with discretion. This is only to be expected. Drug
income is valued first and foremost as a means to project status.
Dealers crave it like the addictive drugs they sell. Status flows
from respect, respect from reputation, and reputation from a conspicuous presence. In violent social worlds, people must prove
who they are *now;* with the end always near, there is no time to
waste (see also Bourgois 1995; Hamid 1998). Personal/nonessen-
tial consumption, flashy demeanor, and stylized posing become
the means to this end (Wright and Decker 1997:40; see also Anderson 1999:29). The problem for drug sellers is that they cannot
pick and choose to whom this message is sent. Status is communicated democratically, attracting the "player haters" they most
want to avoid:

> He was flossing, put it like that. . . . He was showing too
> much. He was representing, like, "I got a lot of money, I got
> a lot of this" . . . showing his stuff off. . . . "I got this, some
> nigger don't got that." . . . Trying to show it off, like, yeah,
> "You ain't got this but look how much . . . I got." So I had to
> get him.—*Crazy Jack*

To have wealth is one thing; to flaunt it in the face of those with
less is another. Deprivation permeates street culture. Those who
floss make its relative nature painfully apparent, sparking envy
and hate (see Duffy and Shaw 2000). Street status, after all, is a

zero-sum game: "If you have something and exhibit it, it means I'm less. Who do you think you are by doing that?" (Anderson 1999:95). The brazen display of wealth therefore becomes a "personal affront that [cannot] go unpunished" (Wright and Decker 1997:141). Esteem is restored only by lashing out (Parrot and Smith 1993):

> Flashing they little money in front of the little gals, counting they money, you know. They holler at they friends. I mean, "You show, partner, I show me about a quarter over today. O.K., quarter over. What about you, partner?" . . . That's a mark. You riding down the street, ain't got no money but you got a pistol, and these niggers standing outside counting they money. [I'm gonna get him.]—*Do-dirty*

> Little dude walked past with jewelry on and stuff, pocket full of money. I was standing on the corner where the [transit] bus run through the little thing and he was walking up the street by a little park right there and I saw him. . . . I don't know him; I know of him. . . . I seen him come around, he driving his little peoples in the car over there riding around. . . . Yeah, I seen him riding in [nice] cars and shit, jewelry, talking to the little girls over there, saw him chilling. . . . That was the person, I was at that place at that right time I guess—*Lil' Player*

> He was a . . . type of guy because he had more than everybody and the way he was talking to my best friend, this and that, I got this and I got that. . . . I just got fucking tired of him talking about all this shit. He gonna show us all this money, this, that, and the other. So there go the ego talking. . . . "You get this nigger, you'll be alright."—*Darnell*

> [Target was] talking shit, . . . like he was on top of the world, . . . [got] an arrogant way about him. Kind of sassy and floss and shit, you know.—*Buck*

Of course, not everyone who talks big, wears fly clothes, or flashes cash is a drug dealer. The widespread adoption of such behavior by nondealers seeking to mimic the look of players may confound accurate identification. To be sure, such persons would occasionally find themselves under the gun. But this did not appear to be frequent. Extensive experience on the streets furnished drug robbers with a finely tuned "perceptual shorthand" (Skolnick 1966). Most had supreme confidence in their ability to distinguish the real from those perpetrating. "You know your dope dealers," Loony Ass Nigga illustrates. "You can tell, I can be certain about 99.9 percent, everybody that walking down my street, I can tell you if they selling dope or what just by looking at the expressions on they faces, . . . watching them move." Such identification was crucial, since drug dealers were targeted for very specific reasons.[3]

The seductive appeal of opportunistic robberies is obvious. They require no real effort; essentially, targets select themselves. Rewards may be unknown, but this makes no matter. The ease of the heist is what counts. (Rewards earned unexpectedly are the sweetest of all; the pleasure of "winning" always is most intense when the outcome is surprising: Mellers et al. 1999:336.) The offenders' unstructured, street-focused lifestyle places them in prime position to capitalize. Most had nothing or no one to tie them down. Life was unscheduled and freeflowing, their day-to-day existence being governed by a volatile mixture of desperation and whims of the moment. Drug robbers were hustlers in the true sense of the term, freed from the constraints of daily obligations and persistently on the lookout for every opportunity to make fast cash (Gould 1967; see also Fields and Walters 1985; Goldstein 1981; Shover 1996). Since the vast majority insisted on never hitting the streets without a firearm, action was a foregone conclusion—provided the right set of circumstances appeared. "I always got a gun so it don't make no difference [what comes my way]," Buck pronounced. "When an opportunity presents itself and I'm ready, I [fly]." As Snap put it, "You don't know when the opportunity gonna jump, [so you always have to be prepared]." "When you got a gun in your hand," Smoke Dog added, "you can get whatever you want. Always remember that. You got a gun in your hand you can get whatever you want." He continued:

I'm gonna tell you like this man. If I leave out of the house today and I see some man with a bird [kilo] . . . and I can get him, I'll get him today. I'll do it today again. It don't make me any day, any time, it don't make me no difference.

Serendipity may be seductive, but over-reliance on it is unwise. Luck is unpredictable. Payoffs and risks are unknown. Victims might end up being "hard targets," something discovered only after the offense is well under way, and thus too late. In committing such offenses, drug robbers are "flying blind"—driven more by faith, greed, and inertia than anything else.

DISCUSSION

Criminologists suggest that targeting strategies are effective indicators of the degree of calculation offenders bring to any crime sequence. Calculation is a function of expertise, expertise a function of accumulated experience in offending. Experts select targets more systematically than their less-experienced counterparts. They demonstrate more advanced intuitive abilities and assess risks and rewards with greater precision (see Khatri and Ng 2000; Kleinmutz 1990; Prietula and Simon 1989). They identify outcome probabilities more accurately and map out contingencies in advance of their occurrence. Generally speaking, expertise is associated with professionalism and professionalism with success (see, for example, Weaver and Carroll 1985).

Drug robbers specialize, and some indeed could be called "experts," but most are far from being the cool, rational professionals their accounts at times imply. Cash-intensive, drug-focused living is not conducive to the consistent application of reason (see Cromwell et al. 1991). Planning may be a good idea in theory, but exigencies of the moment often make it prohibitive. (See, for example, Feeney 1986 on the "casual approach" taken by many armed robbers.) Immediate needs dictate that crude choices be made, often on the basis of limited information. Deadlines—be they real or imagined—exist and must be met. Risks may be downplayed or dismissed altogether (see Bennett and Wright 1984). Or, rewards may be distorted upward to justify taking greater risks. Rational-choice researchers (see Simon 1979) refer to this as "bounded rationality," a necessary but simplifying reaction to complex decision-making demands under time pressure (see also Cornish and Clarke 1986): a "few aspects of a few alternatives are considered and the rest ignored" (Johnson and Payne, 1986:173). Whom one targets becomes less important than *choosing someone;* "aspiration level[s are] set for the selection criteria being used, and the search for alternatives is stopped as soon as the aspiration is met" (Todd 2000:950; see also Simon 1990).

Bounded rationality is not necessarily bad. Shortcuts and rules of thumb can be both expedient and effective, especially in "high-velocity," time-constrained, uncertain environments (Eisenhardt 1989; Khatri and Ng 2000). When strict limits are placed on the relevant factors one can realistically attend to, vital cognitive space is freed up. Psychic loads lighten and focus improves (Cornish and Clarke 1986:11). Information is processed less extensively but with greater accuracy (Eisenhardt 1989). Cognitive economies permit decision makers to ignore irrelevant information and focus squarely on the cues that count (Isenberg 1984; Kirschenbaum 1992; Khatri and Ng 2000; Prietula and Simon 1989). Selection strategies are less comprehensive, but more precise (see Arkes and Ayton 1999:599 on the "fast and frugal" heuristic). Fears and anxieties are more readily shunted from consciousness. This facilitates moments of clarity. And free-flowing decisions lead to a greater likelihood of success; it is not necessarily the quantity of information, but the quality and efficiency with which it is processed that generate desired outcomes (see also Bennett and Wright 1984).

The drug robbers' reported refusal to target dealers they know (and know them) is nevertheless intriguing. It identifies a threshold of risk that all but the most immediate of needs won't allow them to breach. It underscores a capacity for longer-term thinking among those whose lives are driven by instant gratification. It suggests a reluctance to create such acute deficits that bounded rationality is abandoned altogether, or that even in the face of such deficits, some degree of rationality still is possible. It implies that alternative target choices are sufficiently available so as not to force such a choice in the first place. Most important, it highlights the deterrent power of informal sanction threats (i.e., retaliation) in influencing selection decisions. Certain but unpredictable risks are arguably the most powerful obstacle to intended behavior; one knows they are coming, but never when (see also Maher 1997). No amount of hypervigilance can forestall them indefinitely. Besides, worrying is emotionally draining and maintainable at a certain level only for so long.

Until targets become so categorically hardened or inaccessible that quick rewards at low risk can no longer be secured, familiar targets will continue to be avoided, and preparatory work (in the selection process) will remain necessary. Recent anecdotal evidence suggests that this day may be coming sooner than most drug robbers might expect. Emerging studies indicate that street-level dealers are exercising increasing amounts of discretion in both their presentational and distributional styles. Flossing is becoming less extensive and more limited to controlled settings (see, for example, Fleisher 1998:103). Flash is not as vital as it used to be, conspicuous consumption no longer so fetishized a pursuit. The devastating impact of predation on friends, family, and associates has taught many dealers a valuable lesson. "Where drug dealers in the 1980s advertised their success through the purchase of consumer display items, dealers [increasingly are preferring] an understated style, making them, in many respects, indistinguishable from [their nondealing] peers" (Curtis 1999:19). The meaning of high living also has changed drastically in the past few years—in both the type and amount of resources required to support it (Johnson et al. 1990). Dealers are finding it difficult to live up to the material expectations set by prior cohorts, resulting in additional pressures toward discretion.

Changes in distributional styles reduce dealers' vulnerability further still. The threat of arrest and predation is compelling many to restrict sales to a smaller cadre of repeat customers. Others are using beepers to meet clients at predesignated times in public places, high in natural surveillance (for example, grocery stores and gas stations). Yet more are toting only enough contra-

band to complete sales, keeping excess inventory and other seizable contraband off their person.

Of course, dealers can only go so far. As long as legitimate means of status attainment continue to be blocked off, personal nonessential consumption items will be important proxy indicators. Style and social worth is a connection likely to die hard, if it does at all. As for drug market structure, it has been, and in all likelihood will continue to be, freelance in nature: vendors sell for their own individual profit in competition with similarly positioned others for a finite pool of resources. In such a system, interdependence is rare. Sellers are not cohesive enough to establish formal or lasting role structures. Group distribution tends to be haphazard, unstable, and fleeting. Since organization is really the only way to ensure long-term security (Johnson et al. 1992), their prospects do not look good. Individual responses are inherently limited; in fragmentary and competitive markets, accessibility is the *sine qua non* of success. Sellers must be available when customers want to do business. New customers must be cultivated and existing ones lured from other sellers to solidify one's competitive position (Jacobs 1999a). Both involve considerable risk. And high-demand periods requiring large inventories inevitably will persist, resulting in exorbitant losses in the event one is fleeced. Firearm possession is not an option (at least for street dealers), given the steep threat of official sanctions. The opportunity structure for drug robbery does not appear as if it will sour any time soon.

NOTES

1. Excluded from this analysis are targets chosen specifically to punish some past personal affront who, for reasons specified in Chapter 2, select themselves.
2. Compare this to burglary, where offenders prefer to ransack the same target repeatedly (Wright and Decker 1994). Greater familiarity with the dwelling and preexisting knowledge of when victims are likely to be away make them "easy pickings." Theft without contact obvious-

ly brings little if any risk of retaliation later, as long as one's identity can be kept secret.

3. This is not to suggest that nondealers would be bypassed if needs were sufficiently pressing, rewards were perceptibly ample, and the moment felt "right" but rather, that such action reportedly was neither desired nor necessary.

CHAPTER FOUR

Enactment

D RUG ROBBERIES ARE multifaceted enterprises possessing "problematic outcome[s] and potentially serious consequences" (Shover 1991:103). The stakes are high. The moment is heated. Judgment is circumscribed by desperation, emotion, time pressure, and uncertainty. Decisions are split-second and irrevocable. Neither party knows for sure how the other will react. Every move has fateful implications. Critical misreadings threaten outcomes that neither party intends or welcomes. The encounter is interaction in its most primitive form, a Hobbesian stand-off where fear reigns and brute force is the medium of communication.

Success requires that drug robbers marshal and dispense coercive power sufficient to secure cooperation that is both rapid and lasting. This is not easy. Robbery victims are prone to noncompliance—especially drug dealers whose reputations and financial survival hinge on recalcitrance. Losses can be extensive and irretrievable; insofar as the time and effort necessary to recoup them is prohibitive, resistance becomes a foregone conclusion (see Cook 1976). And surrendering without a fight shows weakness in a world where only the strong survive. Reputationally, there are few worse fates.

Force is essential to securing compliance, but using too much can be as bad as using too little. Punitive resources must be managed judiciously lest one undermine the integrity of the offense (see Luckenbill 1981:43). Victims, for instance, might perceive the attack to represent something far more ominous than a robbery or be too stunned to react desirably (Wright and Decker 1997). Either way, the tenability of the robbery frame will be jeopardized. Success, of course, is about much more than the use of force. The overriding issue is control. Each phase of the offense—from approach to announcement to goods transfer—must establish it if drug robberies are to have any chance of success.

APPROACH

Invariably, drug robbers must get close to victims without alerting them that predation is in the offing. At this juncture, surprise is more important than anything else. The conventional nature of the setting must be preserved until the precise moment drug robbers are ready to pounce. To do otherwise is to tip one's hand before any advantage can be secured—creating an unintended state of alert in would-be victims that terminates the offense before it can even begin (see Luckenbill 1981; see also Reidel 1993:148).

Copresence is easy to establish among indiscreet sellers, for many of the reasons specified in Chapter 3, but their skittish counterparts require a good deal more care. "Creeping" was one popular response. The urban topography of St. Louis is saturated with so-called cuts, publicly accessible places that nevertheless remain off the beaten path. Alleys, gangways, dense foliage, and vacant lots provided drug robbers the conduits they needed to sneak up on sellers undetected. They also afforded nooks and crannies into which drug robbers could slip and wait unrevealed for their prey—emerging "out of nowhere" only when ready to strike (see also Wright and Decker 1997:98). Dealers sometimes used the same locales for protection (from the police as well as from predators), which ironically helped to seal the very fate they were trying to avoid:

> I hit the alley, came through the alley, I hopped someone's
> fence, came through the alley and hit his yard, 'cause he
> stands in the gangway when he selling his drugs. . . . So I
> walked up to him . . . I walked up to him and [initiated the
> robbery].—*Bacca*

Even more hardened targets such as houses could on occasion be
made vulnerable by using such measures. Crouching in ground-
cover adjacent to a main doorway, Three Eyes lunged at his victim only after he returned home. "[Catch] them going in," he
explained. "Jump up out of the bush, 'Open your door and let's
go in.'" Indeed, the smallest of breaches could become full-blown
gaps if exploited rapidly enough. "When they open that door,"
Smoke Dog illustrates, "my gun already gonna be aiming . . . aiming at everything. . . . You stick that barrel to they forehead, bing,
walk on in the house." Surprise is critical for placing victims in a
position from which they could not recover. Stunned, victims are
too startled to react, much less resist.

One would expect those at such a high risk of predation (as
drug dealers) to be wise to lurking predators and to prepare accordingly. Awareness, however, need not translate into immunity. Constant exposure to danger causes it to be routinized—as
any participant in high-risk enterprise can tell you. (See Mc-
Sweeney and Swindell 1999:437 on "habituation.") Vigilance is
cognitively taxing and sustainable for only so long; the degree of
psychic energy required is one that most find impossible to maintain (Lejeune and Alex 1973:276). Inasmuch as would-be victims
have been able to avoid negative outcomes in the past, they may
become even more desensitized to risk. "Most guys [dealers],
man, are so [complacent]," Curly claimed, "it makes them an easy
target. They so settled . . . they easy to get, man."

Of course, even complacent sellers can transition to a full state
of readiness if alerted in time. The threat of natural surveillance
was therefore a major source of concern. In general, the streets are
bustling with activity. Bystanders regularly mill about, engaging
in a wide range of social behavior inclusive and exclusive of drug
market participation. Most keep a wary eye on their surroundings,

recognizing the volatile world in which their movements take place. Drug robbers could never really be sure what they might see, how they might react, or if these reactions might tip off those they were targeting.

Most offenders thus insisted on creeping only after dark (see also van Koppen and Jansen 1999). Nightfall provided a natural cloak with which to absorb a stray but incisive gaze, even one that penetrated a cut. Covered in dark clothing, drug robbers could prowl all but undetected. "Night-time . . . that's when I can creep," Goldie asserted, "you know, feel safe." "Never do no robbery in broad daylight," Lewis insisted. "Too many peoples will see you. . . . The best time is at night." "Wear camouflage," Lewis continued, "like military stuff. . . . [Nobody can] see you if you hide in the bushes or you come through the gangway with a black ski mask on."[1]

As a general rule, the later the hour, the more secure drug robbers seemed to feel. Collateral activity declined as a matter of course, providing a more controlled environment in which to operate. "The best times are like 10:30 [PM], 11:00, or 12:00," June Bug remarked, "when traffic kind of slow down." Slim agreed: "[I wait until] about 10:00 or 11:00 at night," he said, "[that's when] things start settling down. Kids [and others] go on in the house, you go and get it off like you want to then . . . ain't got to worry about [no one seeing you]."

Creeping after dark was important for thwarting official detection as well. Though police tend to ride most intensely after dark, offenders seemed to focus more on the ease of being seen than the probability. "I don't want to take a chance of doing it during the day," Spanky insisted. "If you're doing it during the daytime you . . . try to get from one spot to another and the police . . . there. . . . I didn't want the chance of getting [stopped]. . . . At night-time it's like you got a better chance of making it to the spot where you're going." Not satisfied with just the cover of darkness, Curly took the additional step of creating a diversion:

> Set something up three blocks away, create a confusion . . .
> like bust a window or create a disturbance, draw the police

over there. They come and investigate it, so that means they ain't coming up this street here for maybe half an hour, 45 minutes [so I do my thing].

Crazy Jack, meanwhile, became a chameleon of sorts—manipulating his apparel to throw off the authorities in the event he were to come under scrutiny:

> I'll probably have like a white tee shirt on under a black shirt or a green shirt on top, take this shirt off and I'll probably have, like, some basketball shorts on under some regular shorts and take all my clothes off, put some old clothes on top that I don't wear, and then after I hit it [rob the dealer], bang, just throw that stuff away and keep on what I got on.

It would be misleading, however, to suggest that all or even most of the drug robbers were so concerned about formal detection. The majority seemed to dismiss the prospect, believing arrest to be a "remote and improbable contingency" (Shover 1996:102). Drug-focused, cash-intensive lifestyles are not conducive to prolonged worrying. Needs are pressing and require rapid redress. Failure to act when the moment calls for it can result in lost opportunities. The risk of drug robbery is quick anyway, making the threat of official detection perceptibly insignificant. Personal experience with punishment avoidance only fueled a sense of invulnerability felt by many:

> That's [the possibility of arrest is] so freakish. I mean, it's never happened to me.—*Buck*

> Ain't no police around when you robbing no dope dealer. Ain't no police around. They don't ever be around. When you're robbing somebody, when you're getting robbed, they don't ever be around.—*Smoke Dog*

BUYS-TURNED-AMBUSH

A second popular approach tactic was to purchase from would-be victims on one or more occasions prior to robbing them. The idea was to lull dealers into believing subsequent approaches represented nothing more than additional buy-attempts. Suddenly and without warning, drug robbers would transform the encounter into an ambush. "[He thinks I'm gonna buy, but] my mind is another way," Curly declared. "I'm gonna get him" (see also Lejeune and Alex 1973).

As Wright and Decker (1997:98) note, one of the most important prerequisites of any successful street robbery is to "fit into the social setting such that the intended victim perceives the would-be attacker's presence as normal and nonthreatening, thereby allowing [him] to get close enough for a surprise attack." The established customer turned robber presents an unsolvable dilemma. The role of buyer provides an accepted means of establishing copresence, concealing (or at least delaying) exposure of their true intentions. There is little opportunity for dealers to recognize the danger and mount some sort of preemptive strike (Jacobs 1999a:77; Wright and Decker 1997:102–3). It is the classic, perhaps indefensible case of the wolf dressed in sheep's clothing.

"If you, like, go up to them," Crazy Jack explained, "I'm buying from you all, you spending money, you all gonna think I'm a cool guy right? I'm spending money. I'm not out to get over and rob you. . . . The more you keep spending money . . . [the easier it is] to rob 'em." Buck agreed: "You get somebody's confidence, you know, people be comfortable with you coming," he explained. "Then you catch them with they drawers down and you get 'em. . . . Most of the time that's how I get people." "Make them feel comfortable," Snap continued, "they won't get leery, you know. . . . You got to trip their mind, get into they brain, you know." Or, as Curly emphasized, "Only peoples that really can get you, man, are peoples [that get close to you] 'cause you keep your guard down on them. . . . You [researchers] couldn't get me because you a stranger to me, so I'm watching." Disguises, however, could not be worn using this modus operandi, and this was a significant drawback. Other techniques for managing retaliation had to be developed accordingly, tactics discussed in Chapter 5.

As noted in the previous chapter, "set-up buys" might be used to gauge a prospective target's viability—from both a reward and defensibility standpoint. If this information already was known (for example, from observation or inside information), if victims were sufficiently vulnerable, or if drug robbers desired an immediate score, prefatory buys might be bypassed altogether. The frequency with which drug robbers approached victims and attacked them outright suggests that set-up buys, though helpful, were not altogether necessary:

> Crack, he had some dope. They was some 50s [$50 rocks, about one-half gram retail] and stuff like that, though. So I went up to him, I was like, "Let me get a bopper or something." A bopper, that's a $100 pack. He brought it, he was showing me the $100 pack. . . . We was in the gangway. So we was talking. I'm like, "Man, let me get three of them [rocks]," so he brought out three of them. I put the gun up to his head and took it. —*Smoke Dog*

> I had went over there to pretend like I was trying to, the word is "cop," from her. She asked me what did I need. . . . Told her meet me, this was around the corner. So she met me around the corner, so I walked around there and I told her I wanted to get 20. I asked her how big are her stones are and she let me see them. I said, "Well, damn, why don't you just go ahead on and let me get them all," and I pulled my .22 and put it up to her head and . . . told her I want everything she got.—*YoYo*

Victims were often high or drunk, facilitating their exploitation. Historically, the opportunity to party while one "works" has been one of the primary attractions of selling illegal substances (see Inciardi et al. 1993); drug robbers made it a distinct liability. "Why are they easy?" Lewis asked rhetorically. "Because half the time you can catch them blunted out, they done smoked so many blunts [marijuana-filled cigars] and you can walk up and want to purchase something from them and . . . put your pistol to they hip and tell them to come on . . . give me what you got [they ain't gonna do nothing]." Greed only enhanced this vulnerability. Dealers may understand the increased risk that goes hand-in-hand with out-competing other vendors for a finite pool of customers, but most are extraordinarily confident about their ability to avoid consequences. As we all know, awareness of risk need not inspire behavior to avoid it:

> They so money hungry, they have the intention to run to cars, understand what I'm saying? They don't have the patience to wait until a person get out of the car or sit around they friends so that you be secure.—*Blackwell*

> On the streets because you have, they will come to you, you see what I'm saying, like if you pull up or something like that in a car or something like that, they will come to the car to you and will stick their heads up in the window of your car. . . . Once he stick his head in the car . . . you can drive off with him in the motherfucker with half his body hanging up out of there.—*June Bug*

Drive-thru service is a marketing innovation developed during the crack epidemic's expansion phase (circa 1990 in St. Louis; see Hamid 1992 on developmental cycles of drug epidemics). The idea is to raise the volume of available customers, increase the frequency of sales (since buyers with vehicles will tend to have greater financial resources and thus are more likely to come back to buy again), expedite the flow of customers through a selling area, and attract users from outlying venues where hard drugs may be difficult to obtain. Such benefits notwithstanding, drive-thru sales increase sellers' susceptibility in a number of ways. "Protected by locked doors and shatter-resistant windows, buyers [are able to] exploit a clear power asymmetry in the spatial proxemics of the exchange;" they can control their exposure—

"raising and lowering windows, braking and accelerating as they choose" (Jacobs 1999a:71). Body language can be more easily covered, firearms effectively concealed and produced. Sellers, moreover, might actually *enter* a customer's vehicle in the paradoxical search for protection (from police observation). Needless to say, such a move is anything but protective:

> This little dude ... flagged me down. ... He said, "Hey brother, what's up, you looking?" I told him, "Yeah, I'm looking." He said, "What you looking for?" Told him, "I'm looking for some Boy [heroin] and some rock." He said, "All right, look, check this here out. You don't mind if I get in your car?" I told him, "No, come on, get on in there." He said, "Drive around the corner." I take him around the corner; instead of going right around the corner ... jump right on Kingshighway, jump on Highway 70 [so I could rob him].
> —*Do-dirty*

Even cautious street vendors could be lured into copresence, so long as drug robbers signaled interest in subculturally "safe" ways:

> Keep riding around in circles ... keep on circling the block. Like ... ride around the block three times ... ride around, like, three times and then ... circle around ... [study] the thing 'cause [they] get scared when [they] see somebody riding around real slow 'cause [they] think it's like a drive-by or something so they'll hide and then the second time we'll pick up the speed and the man [dealer] will be out and he'll see us and definitely like to buy something, act like [we] want to buy something. ... You don't ride up on somebody looking suspicious 'cause if you ride on somebody like that then they'll think something going down and they leave.—*V-O*

Establishing copresence among house dealers obviously is more difficult. Insofar as participating vendors are insular—

access to them requires familiarity, prefatory buys are not possible, or targeted establishments are too difficult to penetrate—alternative means must be developed. Creeping was one option. Enlisting co-offenders was another. Persons known to, and sufficiently trusted by, would-be victims would be asked to approach the door in a decoy capacity, gain entry, and create a breach. Those lying in wait would then rush the house in a blur of force and threat, establishing copresence and compliance all at once (see also Dietz 1983:58 and Wright and Decker 1997:100):

> When [decoy] open the door . . . when I come up to the door, it's open . . . they [targets] told him to lock the door [but he] don't lock the door.—*Curly*
>
> [Decoy would go up], he would shut the door but the door be open [unlocked]. . . . Don't be wide open, just be shut. —*Goldie*
>
> It's a rush thing. Like if somebody says there is a bomb in the building and everybody runs. That's how it is, it's a rush thing. You got to rush 'em 'cause if you don't you gonna get popped and you got to rush 'em. Either you do or you don't. It's up to you if you want to live.—*Lady Bug*
>
> Ran in the house, we got our guns and bust in the house, the front and back of it, bust in, put everybody on the floor. —*Loony Ass Nigga*

Decoys need not be mandatory, as some of the above anecdotes imply; drug robbers could rush the establishment without them, though entry typically is easier after establishing a beachhead. If decoys were used, it was essential that drug robbers protect their identities, as victims might suspect a setup. Drug robbers might therefore treat accomplices like victims too (for example, "stealing" from them, striking and threatening them, etc.).

The more daunting the target, the more important co-offenders became. And house targets typically are quite daunting. "[They] be ready," Loony Ass Nigga declared. "They know what's gonna happen 'cause it ain't nobody in this world, well I ain't gonna say in the world, but in the dope game, ain't nobody just gonna sit in no house with that much money and that much dope [and not be ready]." Co-offenders permit drug robbers to make the most forceful "announcement" possible and to deter victims from trying to counterattack. For those too intimidated to go it alone, this was extraordinarily empowering. "You a coward when you by yourself," YoYo confessed. "Once you with a crowd you get bigger balls." "I don't ever do it by myself for real," K-red added, "'cause I have a funny feeling [that something might happen]. . . . I have my boys all the time. . . . I ain't by myself." "You got to have somebody with you," Kilo chimed in. "I mean, somebody who gonna back you up" (see also Cromwell et al. 1991; Lejeune 1977; Reidel 1993:146). Teammates, moreover, allowed participants to perform a very specific and limited set of duties, important given the boundedness of their rationality. Role specialization permits focus, and focus is directly correlated with success.

Still, team approaches appeared to be the exception rather than the rule. Much of the reason can be located in drug robbers' deep and fundamental distrust of would-be associates. To claim that street-based relationships are tenuous would be an understatement. Fealty, duty, and solidarity largely are foreign concepts on the streets. One has no friends—only running partners with precarious loyalty. To put one's fate into the hands of another is as unwise as it is dangerous. The risk of being "ratted on" is substantial. As Kilo revealed, "I never took nobody with me or nothing. People get to snitching and what not, you know what I'm saying?" J Rock agreed. "I do it by myself. People will tell on you. . . . I don't trust nobody . . . ain't got no friends in this life. Who got friends [in] this motherfucking life? I know I ain't got no motherfucking friends in life." Blackwell echoed a similar sentiment: "People you take with you, they mostly tell on you. . . . Take a person on a robbery with you, they gonna tell on you and everything." The threat of information leakage was a risk too high to bear for many; if "dirt" was to be done, they would do it themselves. "I would rather just be alone," Lewis underscored, "[then if] anything risky happen, you can't tell on me." Darnell concurred: "I move and groove by myself," he said. "When push come to shove, you ain't gonna tell on your damn self." Or as Ray Ray put it:

> I [do] it by myself 'cause if you do a robbery by yourself it's
> good, you ain't gonna get caught up. You ain't got to worry
> about them looking for nobody else. Like if it's two people
> just did a robbery you all split up, you ain't got to worry
> about your friend gonna tell on you, seeing if he caught. He
> worried about if you caught, thinking about the same thing
> like is he gonna tell on me, I wonder if they catch him if he
> gonna tell on me. Most of the time when you do dirt, do it by
> yourself 'cause you can't get caught up.

For June Bug, the aversion toward team drug robberies was
deeply rooted in experience:

> We did a robbery, like, in '85 and we got, like, some jewelry
> and $15,000 apiece, two rings and stuff, you see what I'm say-
> ing? The Bro [victim] could not identify me or nothing like
> that, but the dude with me told on me and shit, so therefore
> I prefer to be by myself—you see what I'm saying?—'cause
> I'm not gonna go tell on myself.

As early as three decades ago, street offenders were lamenting
the breakdown of the so-called code of honor among thieves.
Shover's (1973:512–13) offenders, for instance, claimed that the
"'solid,' ethical career criminal" was "giving way to the 'hustler,'
an alert opportunist who was primarily concerned . . . with personal—as opposed to collective—security." Though there was
(and continues to be) strong "lip service" to the code, its real-life
influence is quite weak—as modern-day drug robbers attest (cf.
Wright and Decker 1994:76).

Aside from the possibility of being tattled on, one never really
knew what an accomplice might bring—or not bring—to the
table. It goes without saying that would-be accomplices had committed a significant amount of "dirt" exclusive of any current
undertaking. Enlisting co-offenders risked situations that drug
robbers could not prepare for or anticipate. "I don't know what
the next man done did [in the past]," Jay complained. "I could

walk out of here with [him] and there might be somebody looking for [him] and [I] get caught up in the crossfire and . . . [not]
even know what's going on." Moreover, one could never really
know how an accomplice might react *during* the robbery itself;
there is good reason to expect unreliable conduct (Katz 1991:288).
Someone, for example, might "punk out" at a critical moment,
leaving teammates in grave danger. "People can get scared of
anything," Spanky observed. "You know how *you* feel, [but] you
don't really know how the next guy feels." Buck's friend reportedly was shot during a drug robbery attempt because his partner
froze up: "[Victim] had a gun, he had a gun, and the [victim] told
[friend's partner] to put his down and he put it down . . . [and my
friend] got shot." Similarly, Lady Bug's accomplice failed to make
a sufficiently thorough search, with disastrous consequences:

> [My partner] supposed [to] have went upstairs and made
> sure he checked there but he didn't check. He didn't check
> all the rooms like he said he did. The motherfucker [dealer]
> came downstairs, just creep down, and just throw a pop out
> [shot his gun] and I got hit in the leg. . . . My leg was fucked
> up. It took me three years, three years to learn how to walk
> again. I don't even have a bone, that's not even a bone, that's
> a rod and I got pins in there so I have to be careful. . . . They
> tried to amputate this sucker but I ain't gonna let it happen.
> I was determined to walk.

Loony Ass Nigga thus insisted that would-be co-offenders pass a
crude but effective pre-offense litmus test before proceeding with
them:

> Some people, they got some butterflies in they stomach, they
> be scared, you know . . . by me shaking their hand, I feel who
> hand sweating. My father [a violent criminal himself] hip me
> to that. If you hand sweat, I feel out of us, whoever going in
> there, if somebody hand sweating, we ain't gonna do it, be-
> cause I be, like, damn, I didn't pick my people right, you

know. He gonna nut up when he go in there and get us killed
or something.

Obviously, the more people involved, the more complicated
things can get. Signals must be communicated, movements
choreographed, and contingencies accounted for. This is not easy
during the heated moment of an offense, particularly for impulsive, me-oriented street offenders who find it difficult to follow
orders or synchronize behavior with that of associates. Personal
agendas may be followed at the expense of the team, chancing
critical miscues that negatively affect everyone involved. Insofar
as participants are worried about the *possibility* of this occurring,
group performance will be undermined further; anxiety causes
people to "lose focus on achieving the group outcome" as they attempt to cover their behinds by monitoring their partners' actions. This means that only a fraction of their energies will be
directed toward achieving the group goal (Dirks 1999:448).

Finally and perhaps most importantly, team approaches required that proceeds from drug robberies be shared. For many offenders, this was untenable. "I don't want nobody with me," Kilo
insisted, "that's money to split." "You don't do it with a lot of people," Spanky declared, "because that's less for yourself." Revenue
sharing typically was justified only for very large heists; dimin-
ished rewards were an acceptable tradeoff given the perceived
certainty of a greater take.[2] "We got to hit somebody that's got
some money," Crazy Jack declared, "'cause I ain't gonna split no
$200 or $300. You can go rob somebody that got . . . some Gs
[thousands of dollars] or something, got some pot or cocaine
ounces . . . [then it's worth it]." Even then, the pitfalls of working
with others had to be confronted and dealt with.

ANNOUNCEMENT

Like all stick-ups, drug robbery is about control, about how to
secure it as rapidly and as completely as possible. Central to control is the ability to intimidate. Drug robbers must establish in no

uncertain terms who is in charge and what will happen if their orders are not followed. There is perhaps no more important time to do this than when announcing the offense. Robberies are made or broken at their inception.

In announcing the offense, drug robbers "seek to dramatize with unarguable [sic] clarity that the situation has been suddenly and irreversibly transformed into a crime" (Katz 1988:176). "You know what time it is"—a succinct, powerful, and immediately understood phrase—typically opens the interaction. Profanity-laced directives quickly follow to underscore the need for immediate compliance. "Get on the ground, don't move or you're dead motherfucker!" "You got a choice, hand it over or you'll get your [fucking] head blown off!" "Bitch, whore, asshole, motherfucker, up it or else!" and "You come up with anything . . . I'm gonna kill your motherfucking ass" were reportedly voiced with a tone so ferocious and intimidating as to leave no doubt what the victims' next move would be (see also Katz 1988 on the ways of the "badass"). Such commands are "contingent threats"; the victim is informed "that failure to comply . . . will bring the infliction of [injury or death]" (Luckenbill 1980:364; 1981; Tedeschi and Felson 1994).[3]

Being in the "proper mood" was essential to communicating such threats; speaking the words is not enough. Lines must be delivered with verisimilitude sufficient to inspire unmitigated cooperation. "You got to show them that you mean what you're talking about," Bacca illustrates, "show them that you are just out to get what you trying to get and if you can't get it, they got to suffer the consequences." Weakness is easy to spot and impossible to remedy if detected. "You let a person know that you are scared," Baby Doll confessed, "shit, they'll get you. . . . You can't let nobody see."

Not all offenders were equally adept at projecting a badass persona. Some needed a jumpstart. Buck likened himself to a wolverine (an animal he had seen depicted on the Discovery Channel) who, through sheer ferocity, made all antagonists comply. "[He] is a notorious [sic], he is a terrible little guy. I saw him run a bear up a tree. . . . Can you imagine the big old bear running from a little bitty wolverine?" Lil' Player used a method-acting technique of sorts, imagining that "somebody had . . . killed my momma" just prior to the offense. Most, however, turned to the facilitating influence of alcohol and drugs. Pre-offense partying vaporized lingering reservations. Taken in proper amounts, alcohol and drugs disinhibit aggressive tendencies, dissipate fear, and cultivate a capacity for "explosive violence" (see, for example, Berkowitz 1993; see also Katz 1991:288; Lejeune 1977:129). Given the substantial number of robberies committed at the tail end of intensive partying, such effects often came as a matter of course and, indeed, facilitated the decision to do drug robberies in the first place.

"When you are under the influence of drugs," Darnell professed, "you really don't have a sorry word, what the fuck do you care, excuse my French but I'm on the shit, man, I'm flying, you all got this shit so I got to get it." Kilo agreed, claiming that "[Getting high] kind of eases the thing. Drink a little oil [alcohol] or something . . . and just pump yourself up." "I [got] to get high before I go and do this," Goldie concurred, "so my mind just be in another world. . . . So I don't worry about it, you know, whatever happens, happens. I just be in another world."

Some inebriants were seen as more effective than others. But the drug of choice varied from person to person. Crack was the substance preferred by Baby Doll. "When you on that crack cocaine," she mused, "it's just like that crack just make you just, crack will make you do anything, you know, make you do anything and have you feel like you the toughest person in the world. I'm not afraid when I'm high off that crack. . . . It don't matter how big or small [you are], you think you the toughest person in the world. . . . That's the only time I ever do this stuff [drug robbery] is when I'm high or something like that, I'm high." For Bacca, it was heroin. "Heroin . . . makes you feel real strong like you can do anything. . . . [Take] a pill . . . [and it makes] me want to do it [the drug robbery] even more." Smoke Dog spoke of the insane mentality heroin allegedly produced, a mentality ideal for perpetrating violence. "[Snort] me one of them pill things," he said, "and . . . just [go] crazy then."

There is, of course, a real danger of overdoing pre-offense partying. Blunted judgment can cause risks to be dismissed or mistakes to be made. Given that drug robberies often entailed a desperate attempt to continue wild bouts of partying, real problems might be in the offing. "If you high or drunk," V-O revealed, "then you can slip up, mess up." Loony Ass Nigga and June Bug were more expansive:

> You can't concentrate right. 'Cause like when you drunk it's careless mistakes. You got to be so careful of anything 'cause if you don't you may go in there, fall or something, trip over and fall or something on your gun and shoot your partner or let your gun fall and let somebody else get it. . . . You might go in the house and throw up, you know what I'm saying, and then that's your life.

> Smoking cocaine it be geeked all up, playing with your nerves and you gotta wait till you settle, until you come down to your right frame of mind. . . . Don't nobody that smoking rock cocaine be in their right frame of mind because it's a speed high so therefore you have to sit and wait until you come back down because you be up there on a high level so you got to wait until you come back down on your level before you do anything.

Offenders typically announced the offense and brandished firearms coterminously. There is nothing more ominous than having a loaded gun shoved in one's face and being ordered to comply on the threat of death. Intimidation, after all, is about fear, and few things create it more convincingly than the specter of lethal force. Guns can kill, they can kill impersonally from a distance, and they leave little chance for a counterattack; "because everyone knows that a gun has these attributes, [its] mere display . . . communicates a highly effective threat" (Cook 1982:247).

"When you got a gun in your hand," Smoke Dog pronounced, "you can get whatever you want. Always remember that." "Ain't too much they gonna say cause they don't want to tick you off," Jay added. Kilo concurred, claiming that "once people see the gun, they pretty much fold, you know. . . . I mean, if I told you to give me your watch you would probably say 'fuck you.' If I pull a gun on you you'd probably say 'fuck you' but [you would] give it up." According to Darnell, "It's either give [me] this shit or die. . . . [Victims know] what time it was." With the "ups" on someone else, there is nothing to do but comply:

> When a person got a . . . loaded automatic in his hand. What type of fool gonna make a mistake like that so he can get killed for some money? So why not just go on and give the person what the fuck he wants, let the person get the fuck away, understand what I'm saying?—*Blackwell*

> Pull a gun . . . and he can't do nothing but do what [I] say unless [he] want to die. It's so easy to rob. . . . It's so easy to rob people. Somebody pull a gun out, they ain't gonna move cause they don't want to die. They gonna let you do what they got to do, check 'em, go through they wallet, purse, anything, look through the house, look for the crack, the dope. Ain't nobody gonna move, nobody, 'cause don't nobody want to die.—*Crazy Jack*

Minimal necessary force is perceptual, and a few drug robbers insisted on toting multiple firearms. "I always carried two guns when I was going to do anything," Curly explained. "I didn't think one was sufficient. . . . See, two guns will scare them more . . . put something on they mind. If you got two guns you ain't bullshitting. . . . He not gonna go against these pistols, he's caught." June Bug and Ray Dog agreed:

> I always like to have two because no telling who might run up in that motherfucker, you see that I'm saying? 9's [Nine mms] shoot 18 times apiece, you see what I'm saying? That's a lot of shots man, you see what I'm saying? I mean, that's enough to keep any motherfucker off you, man.

> You got two pistols . . . cocked, fully loaded . . . one in your mouth and one in your head what you gonna say? What you gonna do? Can't do nothing else but do what I tell him to do.

The number of firearms, however, seemed to be less important than their type. Most respondents preferred the biggest, baddest, and most fearsome-looking gun possible. Ugly weapons—old, scratched, pock-marked from years of dirty work—were especially favored. The uglier and more intimidating the gun, the less likely the drug robbers would have to use it. "I don't want a pretty gun," Buck illustrates, "[I want it] big, black, and ugly. . . . [That] keep[s] you from having to hurt somebody." The weapon of choice for many was a .45. "When they see that big old .45 with that 9-inch barrel on her," Do-dirty exulted, "they bags up, they bags up." Slim agreed:

> They [.45s] big, they ugly, and they shoots good. . . . Just pulling it out and staring down in the barrel of that pistol, that's enough to give you something to think about, that's what make it so ugly. . . . When you take it and put it up to his mouth and let him bite down on it with his teeth and just talk to him, he gots to [give in], you know.

Nine mms and .357 magnums followed close behind. June Bug reveled in the sheer firepower of the nine. "They shoot good . . . knock their motherfucking brains against that wall, knock his brain out of the wall." Darnell concurred: "A nigger see one of those and shuts the fuck up. I shut the fuck up when I see one." Smoke Dog preferred his .357 magnum: "It's big and it kick," he boasted. "I like guns that kick when I shoot 'em. They give that little pow, like that, that kick, you know what I'm saying? That's my baby, I love that magnum, I swear I do, I love it." Smoke Dog and others talked about their weapons with all the joy and exhilaration of a young child on Christmas morning; their faces "glisten and brighten . . . their bodies inflate like a gas balloon. Their backs straighten and limbs stiffen; excitement and passion overcome them" (Fleisher 1995:57).

Not all offenders trumpeted the merits of big, powerful guns. Some considered them too bulky and burdensome, as well as counterproductive to approaches reliant on stealth. The bigger the weapon, the more difficult it was to hide and the more prone it was to being exposed prematurely. "I ain't going nowhere with no shotgun or no AK or nothing, [not even a] 9mm," Crazy Jack explained. "[I take a .32 automatic] 'cause it [is] so small and I [can] walk with it. A little handgun you can put in your pocket and walk and then if you have to run it ain't that big, you can run with it." Placed inside the front waistband of one's pants, covered by a baggy shirt, small guns were virtually undetectable. "[Can't walk] around with a bigass .357 under my shirt [and] catch 'em off guard," Kilo admitted. "[By contrast,] I could probably have a .25 in my pocket now and you wouldn't know anything." Lady Bug concurred:

> Why would I walk down the street with a big old long gun? They don't need to see what I got in my hand. They don't know what I want. That's how you do it. You walk up on them. . . . When I walk, you don't know what I got.

Reduced firepower did not necessarily make drug robbers less potent. Small guns can produce mortal injuries nearly as easily as their larger brethren. "A gun is a gun," Kilo reasoned. "I wouldn't want to get shot with one. [In fact,] a lot of people say .22s and .25s are like murder weapons because the bullet travels. You can get shot in the knee and it end up in your gut." Bacca agreed, claiming that the .25 bullet would go through the victim's whole body, puncturing internal organs before stopping. Firearms were firearms; it all came down to the skill of the shooter in using them—if, indeed, shooting became necessary.

VICTIM RESPONSE

Many victims reportedly had a strong tendency to disbelieve what was happening to them. "What you doing, what you doing?" Smoke Dog reported one dealer asking him incredulously. "Robbing you. . . . What it [look] like I'm doing?" Jay recounted

similarly: "[Victim] told me I was tripping. . . . 'No I'm not tripping, you tripping.'" Or as Kilo observed: "I told him to give me
all of [his shit] and he was like, 'Man, what the fuck you doing?'
He don't think I was real at first."

Hesitation is a natural reaction to the sudden loss of autonomy
(see Brehm and Brehm 1981; Lejeune 1977; Lejeune and Alex
1973). "Momentarily shocked and disoriented, the victim [fore-
goes] routine action in order to determine whether the move
should be taken as a sign of a prank or exploitation" (Luckenbill
1981:33). Shock can provide a distinct advantage for drug robbers. The greater the disorientation, the lower the risk of resistance, and the more rapidly they can realize their objectives:

> Man, he was like, he was so shocked that we came up to him
> that he just, we took the money, he had the money and
> we took it. We had ran and we took it. He just like, "damn."
> —*K-red*

Yet surprise also can create unintended delay as victims struggle
to reorient their perceptions (see Lejeune 1977). The more time it
takes between announcement and goods transfer, the less control
drug robbers have. Delays suggest a lack of compliance that, if allowed to persist, threaten to undermine the integrity of the offense. Insofar as hesitation mutates into resistance, even greater
problems are in the offing.

Delays were not uncommon. Most dealers are accustomed to
the threat that goes hand-in-hand with selling illicit drugs. Many
have had violent confrontations in the past, escaping injury or
death only by being cool under fire. On the streets, recalcitrance
in the face of threat is essential; its dramaturgic value increases in
direct proportion to the threat's perceived lethality. "You got
some people like that," Jay explained. "'I'm not gonna give up
shit, I ain't giving you shit man, fuck you.' You got some people
like that."

Hesitation typically was a stalling maneuver intended to break
the drug robbers' resolve. Victims might also use the opportunity

to make threats of their own—"I'm gonna get you and this and that, all this and that [Kilo]"—but usually they attempted to talk aggressors out of completing the offense, either explicitly or implicitly. Drug robbers needed to respond accordingly, lest they lose the advantage they had labored so diligently to create:

> He [dealer] kind of hesitated a minute. Man, this is bullshit. . . . He was stalling. . . . I was contemplating shooting him but I didn't. . . . Like, motherfucker, the more you talk to them really, the more probably the situation will escalate into something that you don't want it to be. He'll probably figure that he can reason with you or some shit, you know what I'm saying? You just don't say nothing to him. Like I said, I told him to give it up and I kept a gun in his face and I didn't take my eyes off of him.—*Kilo*

> They crying, "Please man, please man," they kind of get on your nerves. You might want to smack them and tell them to shut up or something because that can mess with your head while you doing it. Crying, "Oh my momma," and all this, "Gonna miss me," and all that, shut up, shut up, and just get on the ground, let's get this over with.—*Loony Ass Nigga*

Victims might also use the opportunity to explain (retroactively) what they would have done had a gun not been jammed in their face. "You could have just asked me for some dope or money and I would have gave it to you," was the modal attempt. The transparency of such efforts made most drug robbers bristle with anger. "[You] wouldn't have gave me [nothing]," Spanky reportedly replied in one such encounter. "Fuck you." Darnell retorted similarly: "Fuck, when I ask I don't get it. So I have to go through the pistol to make you niggers understand."

Kilo insisted that one could avoid the perils of hesitation by using force proactively; he announced one offense by pistol-whipping the victim:

> I came up behind him. . . . Hit him, hit him with the pistol. . . . Strike 'em. . . . Just smack him with the butt of the gun, you

> know, in the back of the head somewhere . . . and told him he
> had to give it all to me, I wanted it. I wasn't gonna let him
> move around. . . . He handed [the drugs] to me. . . . He didn't
> try nothing funny. I guess he [was] . . . scared.

The vast majority of offenders, however, dispensed brute force only to *reestablish* control (see also Lejeune 1977). Punishment produces pain, and pain engenders immediate compliance (on pain cues, see Tedeschi and Felson 1994:368). "I told him this is a robbery," Blackwell recounted, "he tells me 'this ain't no robbery. You ain't taking nothing from me,' so I hit him on the side of the head, let him know I wasn't playing." "I ain't giving you nothing," Do-dirty recalled another victim telling him. "All right, you don't give me nothing. OK, well here, check this here out, pow [striking the victim]. Now what you gonna do?" "If he even trip," Curly continued, "smack him to let him know you ain't bullshitting. . . . Whip him with the gun. . . . Put the ouch on him, man." Or, as Jay put it, "I have to hit him upside his head with the pistol. After I hit him three or four times then he [know I] was all serious." Smoke Dog put it similarly: "[Smack him] to let him know I ain't playing with him. That's just to let him know. You got to do it. You talking to somebody, you gonna mess around and smack him with it or you gonna shoot him."

Darnell, meanwhile, preferred to "Sho[o]t . . . at the ground a few times, let him know I [am] not bullshitting." Three Eyes and Blackwell claimed that warning shots were not enough. "I'll shoot 'em in the arm, leg, knee, just to let you know that I ain't playing," said the former. "[But] next time it won't be one of them little parts that you can survive without." Blackwell reportedly shot his victim in the leg twice when he failed to hand over the goods in a prompt manner. "He shouldn't have took that long to give it to me," Blackwell insisted, "damn near a minute and a half."

Others chose to displace their wrath onto copresent third parties. Insofar as the safety of a victim's relative or close friend is credibly threatened, swifter responses might be in order. "See, if I put a pistol in a kid's head," June Bug pointed out, "his momma will do anything in her power to serve me and to do whatever

I want her to do you know. 'I don't care about you killing me, just don't kill my son,' you see what I'm saying? 'You let my son live.'" Ray Dog used this very tactic, threatening to kill a recalcitrant victim's infant son if he continued to disobey:

> So we were asking him about where the dope at in his house, where's the dope at? He claims he don't know where the dope at. I grabbed the boy's baby and put the pistol at the baby head. I said, 'Where the dope at?' Then he claimed he don't know where the dope at. Cocked the pistol. 'Where the dope at, man, because you know I don't mind killing this baby.' But at the same time I ain't gonna kill his baby, man, I'm just putting fear in his life. But that been a grown person, yeah, a baby, a baby ain't got nothing to do with this here because the baby don't know what's going on. It just there because it's daddy there, it's daddy and momma in the house. So after I cocked the pistol and told him what I was gonna do, you dig, he said, 'Over there, man, right there.' 'Where the money at?' 'The money over there.' Telling his wife, go get the dope, go get the money. Walk through the house with the baby like this here. You letting him know, you see what I'm saying? The joke is over with the dude. "I done asked you two times where the money and dope at, you know, but you was steady bullshitting. I'll try to show you something, take your pride and joy from you. I'll kill your kid. I'll take your kid's life."

Whether meted out against dealers or related third parties, most drug robbers found the use of force to be intrinsically rewarding (on intrinsic motivation, see Eisenberger et al. 1999). Domination and control over someone else's fate brought enormous pleasure to those whose lives were, in many ways, spinning out of control. "Just seeing the motherfuckers doing what you tell them to do, you know," Goldie beamed, "get down, and they get down and shake a little. They be scared that I'm gonna kill 'em or something." Or as Jay Rock put it, "You lay the motherfucker down on the ground and beg for his motherfucking life [makes me feel good]." "I like seeing the fear," Snap gloated. "I like seeing people scared, I like seeing that." June Bug claimed that he got his "thing on watching motherfuckers . . . scream, crying, begging, 'Don't kill me!' It's fun to me. 'Hey man, please don't hurt me.'" Do-dirty, meanwhile, loved seeing victims "shake in they pants. I seen a dude shit and piss on his self," he recalled with obvious glee. Offenders felt more secure about themselves by exposing weakness in others. This is not surprising; status is a function of the ability to dominate others, which permits the "thrilling demonstration of personal competence"—invaluable, no matter how fleeting it may be (Katz 1988:9; see also Zimring and Zuehl 1986 and Toch 1969 on the "recreational" nature of violence).

In nearly all cases, however, offenders endeavored to avoid killing their victims. Lethal violence may be the best way to quell resistance, but it is far from desired. Bodies bring heat and negate a primary reason why these offenders rob drug dealers in the first place: because they cannot go to the police. Underworld victims may not truly be victims, that is, unless or until they are killed (see Kroese and Staring 1993 on the "moral boundaries" of violence; see also Gabor et al. 1987:61). "You kill somebody," V-O explained, "that's . . . 14 years of your life [in prison]. You don't want . . . that." Buck agreed: "[Drug] robbery is all about intimidation. . . . We don't really want to [kill] nobody. . . . We will but we just coming for the money, that's all." The idea, then, is to establish fear in the psyche of the victim. To do so is to unnerve them and sufficiently weaken their propensity for resistance. This is particularly important for the safe and efficient transfer of goods.

GOODS-TRANSFER

Drug robbery is a sequential offense and with each step, the consequences become increasingly irrevocable. The sequence reaches its climax at the point where goods are transferred. At this time more than any other, victims become unmistakably aware that they and their valuables are about to be separated. If one were going to resist, this would be the time to do it.

Sheer proximity increased the chance that some unexpected move might be misread by drug robbers or not detected in time, with potentially fatal consequences. Methods of exchange had to be devised accordingly. These methods typically varied by enactment context. In house robberies, for example, offenders would usually immobilize victims before conducting a search. Three Eyes thus hustled his victims to the floor and forced them to lie in a "corpse-like state" (Katz 1988) before rifling through the dwelling:

> The ground more safer, you know what I'm saying, than them trying to jump up off the ground and try something with me. Hey, I'll tag your ass on that ground real quick, you know what I'm saying? . . . Put a gun in the motherfucker's face and say, get your ass on the ground.

Buck went a step further, using a loop-knotting technique he reportedly learned in the navy to "rodeo wrap" his victims' hands and feet together. Others used power or telephone cords for the same purpose, duct-taping their victims' mouths so that they remained both immobile and silent. The time spent doing this reportedly outweighed the extra threat of detection that went with prolonged exposure at the enactment site. It facilitated escape as well:

> Dope robberies man, you see what I'm saying, the mother-fucking people get to hollering and screaming, you know, motherfucker get to screaming and hollering, if a mother-fucker in a house with (inaudible), it's gonna be all tension. If the motherfucker trying to make it to the door get to hollering, you see what I'm saying? . . . So I'm gonna put duct tape around their mouth and around their hands and stuff and I'm gonna walk up out of there.—*June Bug*

In the offenders' favor was the fact that the goods transfer could usually be made rapidly. Contraband often was in plain sight, minimizing the need for search time. Offenders typically brought sacks with them. After securing compliance, it became a simple matter of grab, bag, and run:

> I was grabbing the stack of money, all the money. He had them stacked where you could grab it. He was stacking his money, counting it. So I just grabbed it, bing, bing, bing, put it in my pocket. Left up out of the house I had dope in my pocket, some pocket, dope in this pocket and money in this pocket.—*Smoke Dog*

> Everything we needed was right here in this one room, everything on the table. . . . We just grabbed everything . . . money . . . dope, weed, they straps [guns] was sitting out, you know. So we got the straps, the money, I got to check in they pockets, taking they jewelry off, everything. [Got over $3,000 worth of stuff altogether].—*Loony Ass Nigga*

Even if hidden, stashes usually could be found in "obvious" places such as inside cupboards, closets, crawl spaces, under mattresses, or beneath floorboards. Experience and intuition—after all, many drug robbers were or had been dealers themselves—taught them where to search first:

> We was going in for something, you know, look in the least expected places and you also gonna look where I would normally and you would normally just keep some: in your closet, up under your mattress, up under the bed, you know. Motherfucker have a safe . . . in his closet up under some clothes and shit like that . . . you know, the little safe that you probably get at K-Mart or something, you know, with the little key to it. . . . So we just grabbed it. . . . We took it to our house and we all sat around the table and took our time trying to get the motherfucker open.—*Three Eyes*

> Well, when you come in the house there is like a closet, it's not a closet, it's a water heater and where the water heater goes up it's a square hole in each wall, every apartment. He kept it up there on the side; it's like a little attic up in there. —*Bacca*

Up under some mattress . . . pulled up a little wood thing and
in a little box he had like stashed there. Like, he had a wood-
en floor, stashed in the wooden floor. . . . It was, like, four
ounces [of heroin] . . . [an] ounce of cocaine [and] $10,000.
—*Darnell*

Curbside dealers, by contrast, typically retained their drugs "off
premises"—off their person—usually in some secret, street-
based stash spot. Such spots generally would not be more than
several feet from their owner (to allow rapid restocking) and typically in line of sight, but ensconced in such a way as to prevent
identification. Some were wrapped in paper and buried in soil
nearby, with a uniquely shaped twig, mound of earth, penny, bot-
tle, or cigarette butt placed over the top to mark it. Others were
put in soda cans and deposited in dumpsters, on top of building-
ledges, inside hollowed spaces of trees, or in bushes with paper
draped over them (Jacobs 1996b:371). Through careful observation, drug robbers could determine their location—if not precisely, at least generally, which usually was good enough. "I [may
not] know where the dope is," Smoke Dog confessed, "but . . .
they . . . don't keep running back there [behind a building] for
nothing. Nobody just gonna keep running to no back way piss-
ing every three minutes or something, ain't gonna piss that
much. . . . They got some dope back there [and I'm going to
find it]."

As Smoke Dog implies, tactical errors committed by would-be
victims facilitated the discovery of stashes. J Rock recalled a seller escorting him into an alley to complete a transaction, revealing
the all-important hiding place in the process. "That's stupid," he
remarked. "That's on him. That's why he got got, motherfucker,
stupid motherfucker." Selling and restocking one's inventory in
too close proximity was an error with similar consequences:

All right. Me and one of my little partners, right, we rolled
up. I mean, I smoke weed. Let me get a sack of weed from
him, right? And so the dude gave me a sack and he had a
whole bunch of sacks in back by the trash can, up under the

trash can. . . . So I went on over there and while he selling me the sack, the weed, all the time I was gonna rob him. I ain't gonna buy no weed from him, I'm gonna rob him. And so I caught him when he bent down going to his bag. He had at least about 40-some sacks in there. . . . That's $400 strong, $400 strong.—*Smoke Dog*

Such errors also could be induced, as Smoke Dog proved by luring his victim into a gangway under the pretext of police surveillance:

"Why don't you-all step in the alley, man, 'cause it's too hot to be standing right here. The police might ride up or something. Why don't we go in the gangway?" That was stupid. You don't never supposed to show nobody where you keep your dope at. . . . He had some dope in a brick like, you know, them bricks, them cement bricks? . . . He had broke a brick down so he could flip a brick over. You know how you pick up a brick and there be a lot of bugs and all that stuff under there? There was some rocks [crack] up under there, some dope, he had all dope up under there. So . . . I peeped it and I took it.

Blackwell pulled a maneuver that brought the stash *to* him—requesting a rather large purchase amount that compelled the target to return with the entire inventory, which Blackwell expressly intended to (and did) snatch:

[Drive up,] you tell them what you want and they'll say, "Well hold on, let me go back and get what you want, I [don't] got enough of it [on me]." Then they go get they whole stash. Then they bring the whole stash to the car [and I up the gun].

Insofar as victims were able to deposit the stash somewhere on their person before drug robbers could seize it, problems might have arisen. Drug robbers could not really trust victims to hand over the goods, given the opportunity this provided to make a false move. "[Victim] got to reach down and dig all in there to get the money [and drugs]," YoYo remarked. "I don't know if she gonna pull out a gun or the money. . . . She could be reaching for what she want to get . . . and then therefore I got, got." Yet conducting the search oneself required that victims be constrained and the loot secured all at once, not an easy task: The closer drug robbers got to their victims, the more vulnerable their weapons were to being jarred or seized. "I didn't want to go through his pockets," Lil' Player recalled, "'cause if I would have went through his pockets I wouldn't have had a good enough grip on him. If I would have went in his pockets, he could have did something to me. He could have reversed or anything."

Reversals did indeed happen. One of Buck's victims suddenly grabbed the barrel of his pistol—at which time Buck's partner was compelled to open fire.[4] Lewis, meanwhile, reportedly was forced to flee when a victim clutched at the ski mask he was wearing, nearly pulling if off, while shrieking for assistance at the same time. "I had no alternative but to run," he lamented. Loony Ass Nigga claimed that eye contact was the key to detecting incipient resistance and heading it off before any damage could be done:

> You really ain't got to watch they hands, just look at them in they eye. Just keep your eyes on his, when you see him, just give me everything, keep your eyes on them 'cause if they eyes get to flinching, always tell people if they get to flinching they eyes they gonna try something. They either gonna up [pull a gun], they gonna up on you, either, or. 'Cause ain't nobody like being robbed, that's too much money. They know that's a lot of money getting took away from them man. They don't like that, they'll kill you for that if you drop [your eyes].

Most offenders insisted on training their weapons, finger-on-trigger, directly on some part of the victim's body (preferably the head, neck, or back) as they obliged him or her to produce the goods. Drug robbers could then "devote their undivided attention to watching for signs of danger" (Wright and Decker 1997:108). Any sudden movement would result in swift and severe consequences. "If you make any type of false mistake," Blackwell recalled telling a dealer, "I'm gonna shoot you right on the spot." Do-dirty, similarly, informed his victim that if "you move I'm gonna pop you, I'm gonna shoot the shit out of you." Ray Ray claimed he might take the additional step of putting "it [gun] in they mouth or something. 'You think I'm bullshitting, I'll blow your fucking head off.' Put it in they mouth or something, put it in they ear or something, let 'em know you ain't playing."

When possible, drug robbers insisted on making their victims strip. Though street-based victims may be disproportionately unarmed (and thus "soft"), taking this for granted could have disastrous results. "This . . . big old fat-ass nigger," Darnell recalled, "he used to hide a little Derringer [a very small pistol] in his navel. It look like nothing and then he'll probably pull out a gun and pop me in my head. So I took him in the alley and made him take off all his clothes." The manifest function of stripping, however, was to ferret out undiscovered contraband. Underwear was a popular on-person stash spot; dealers commonly cloistered drugs/money inside a secret crotch-pocket located in most brand-name briefs (Jacobs 1999a). "'You got some Skippies on?'" June Bug recalled asking a victim. "'Turn around and let me see if you got some money down there,' 'cause they hide money all in they drawers and shit." Footwear and pants were popular locations as well. "[Make] him strip, take his clothes," Curly observed, "'cause he [past victim] had money in his shoes and his socks . . . and he had money everywhere, man, all in his drawers and shit." Or as Darnell observed, "[They keep] maybe $20 or $30 [in their pocket] but in his shoe he have a bundle of money." June Bug agreed: "Dope dealers hide money all in their shoes. 'Take them Nikes off, motherfucker; I know you got some money [in them].'" Ray Dog, meanwhile, paid special attention to slacks:

> They got they pockets sewed up, other pockets sewed up on the inside of their clothes. They keep all types of money and jewelry inside they clothes hid, sew pockets on the inside. So

> you could take a pocket like this here and turn it inside and
> then down below up on here is another pocket like this here
> and turn it inside and then down below up in here is anoth-
> er pocket that's been made up in there, you can't even tell it's
> up in there. And you might hit that pocket and you might
> come out of there with $3,000 or $4,000 in that pocket.

It was important, however, not to sacrifice safety for the sake of
being thorough. Insofar as thoroughness is fueled by greed, drug
robbers ran the real risk of having their attention diverted in
offense-ending ways. Time and threat, moreover, are directly correlated, and the marginal utility of extra rewards simply was not
enough to justify an extended stay. "I got what I was concerned
with," Buck recounted of a past robbery. "You want to do it . . .
and move on. . . . I don't know who else might be coming."
"That's more time wasted," Goldie observed. "It's about time. . . .
That's too much time and it might not be no other stash. . . ."
Spanky concurred: "I [don't] want to be greedy. I just want . . . to
get what I [can get] and get out. . . . Never be greedy . . . [go in
to get more] and probably never come back out." Or, as Darnell
declared, "Greedy get you caught up. I'm just here to get what I
can get."

Though offenders tried to choose times and places that presented the lowest possible risk, both street and house locations
are venues where activity is not stifled for long. The wisest course
of action is to seize as much as one can as rapidly as possible, and
then leave. As long as the cache is close to what one expected to
secure, there is little cognitive dissonance in leaving undiscovered contraband behind. As one of Wright and Decker's (1994:144)
burglars aptly remarked, "You miss a lot, but it's all gravy if you
get away." Kilo echoed this sentiment:

> I just figured, I mean I saw the [heroin] pills and I knew it was
> a lot of pills, you know what I'm saying? I figured this is the
> lick. I saw him when he gave me the bag and the bag was full.
> It was about half the size of my fist balled up full of pills and
> I knew it was a lot. I knew I did good and I just ran after
> that. . . . It's for the needy, not the greedy.

Not being greedy is important for managing retaliatory risks as well. Darnell, for example, robbed a big-time house dealer of $10,000 in cash and several thousand dollars' worth of drugs, but reportedly left without taking *all* of the booty. This led him to claim that he really "didn't hurt [the victim] 'cause if I did, I could have gotten more out of the deal which I knew there was more there. . . . I see the guy to this day. He might smile. . . . And to this day, I don't think I really hurt him." Similarly, Ray Ray *returned* a diamond ring to a victim before leaving the scene. "'I ain't gonna do you like this,'" he reportedly told the seller. "'You can have at least one ring back.'" Such overtures, however, clearly were more the exception than the rule. Nonetheless, it must be underscored that in these communities—and in drug markets writ large—predation is so common as to be measured in degrees. Insofar as drug robbers are able to moderate the amount they steal, victims might be more likely to "write off" the loss and move on. Given the speed with which sellers (at least resourceful or well-connected ones) can replenish lost inventory / cash, such a strategy may be well grounded.

ENDING THE OFFENSE

Where one escaped to typically was less important than how quickly one did it. The modal plan was to run from the scene as fast as possible, training weapons on victims until the last available moment. Escape from house robberies required perhaps the most vigilance, given the rapidity with which dealers might react after gaining liberty from their attackers:

> I had my partner in the car start it up. . . . I'm still looking [up at the house]. I'm by the car with the door open. I'm just waiting on him to start it up and get it off the ground. So I'm still looking up at the house. They ain't gonna run to the door 'cause if they do then I would have had to start shooting.
> —*Loony Ass Nigga*

The importance of clearing the house of weapons before escaping becomes obvious:

> I was trying to find a pistol because you never know once you rob somebody in they house I guarantee they might have a pistol come back shooting at you. . . . I got the stuff. Then I told her "Stand at the door," and I kept pointing the pistol at her until I got down the steps and once I got down the steps we ran and jumped in the car.—*Crazy Jack*

Escapes typically are made with admonitions not to move, yell, or call for help for several minutes. Such directives often are supplemented by additional verbal harassment, as if to flaunt in victims' faces that they had gotten their way and there was nothing they could do about it. "Punk ass nigger, fuck you all up," illustrates Smoke Dog. A number of offenders insisted on communicating parting words to victims that vaguely suggested future contact. "I'll holler at you, man," or "I'll be back for your ass in a minute" (J Rock) were examples. On the streets, such comments translate into, "I'm going to rob you again," or "I'm going to get you before you get me first." They are intended to extend the illusion of impending threat beyond the actual drug robbery, and to deter retaliation by instilling lasting fear (see also Wright and Decker 1997). Whether they succeed in doing so is another matter and beyond the scope of the present study.[5]

DISCUSSION

Conduct norms in predatory encounters are based on taken-for-granted assumptions of anticipated behavior. Offenders and victims are co-oriented, working from a common situational definition that coordinates actions into a joint performance (Luckenbill 1981:25). Reciprocity creates mutual expectations that permit encounters to proceed with minimal conflict (Reidel 1993:144). In many ways, stickups have an "etiquette," and when both parties enact it, offenses "can resemble a ballet in which each side smoothly performs a choreographed part" (Anderson 1999: 126, 128).

Yet there is a "ubiquity of suspense" that plagues the offense from inception to completion. Victims are unsympathetic and not inclined to comply for long. Enduring consensus comes only through forced compliance. "High-intensity terror" projects indominability and with indominability comes sustained control (Reidel 1993:155–59).

Obviously, the use of force must be measured, as victims might "fatefully misread" the attack to represent something far more serious than a robbery (Katz 1991:285; see Wright and Decker 1997). Misattribution is a very real possibility in the face of acute distress. Time pressure and uncertainty undermine effective cognitive processing (Felson 1978). If harm, for example, is predicted no matter how one reacts, furious resistance becomes not only logical but essential (Wright and Decker 1997:106–7; see also Katz 1988). Drug-robbery victims have a reservoir full of hostility expectancies anyway, and may be intoxicated at the time of victimization (see Dodge and Newman 1981 on the notion of expectancy). Many, moreover, are willing to risk more to have a chance of losing less, particularly when contraband is valuable and / or difficult to replenish: The anticipated "sunk costs" create so much cognitive dissonance that resistance becomes the only realistic response; no amount of indominability will deter those who perceive everything to be on the line, and nothing to lose (see also Arkes and Ayton 1999; Kahneman and Tversky 1979; Moessinger 2000; Tedeschi and Felson 1994).

The dramaturgical salience of resistance goes unstated. On the streets, reputation is everything (Anderson 1999). Reputation flows from competence and competence from the display of recalcitrance in the face of threat (Jones and Pittman 1982; Maher and Daly 1996; Tedeschi and Felson 1994). Anything short of noncompliance, even if merely symbolic, can be enormously damaging and cycle back to create even worse outcomes in the future. As one long-time drug seller put it, to give in is to make "everybody and anybody ... [think] they [can] take something from [you]. There ain't no way possible for you to sell drugs and survive if [people think] they can . . . just come and rob you at will and you not gonna do anything about it." By responding, victims convince predators, past and future, to displace their activity onto softer targets more likely to give up without a fight.

Yet in the face of noncompliance, or at least its potential, drug robbers do not have the option of abandoning the offense, even if another target is readily available. Practically and reputationally speaking, anything short of follow-through is unacceptable (see also Katz 1988:190; Katz 1991:287). Their reported reluctance to use deadly force is a bit hard to believe against this backdrop, particularly if it is grounded in formal sanction fears, as they say. These offenders target drug dealers precisely because the police don't care what happens to them. Even murdered vendors are unlikely to elicit a vigorous response; "dirtbags" and "shitbums" deserve whatever fate befalls them (see, for example, Klinger 1997). Left alive, such persons bring an enormous risk of retaliation. Payback is moot if aggrieved parties are eliminated; friends and associates cannot be relied on to pick up the retributive slack—no matter what offenders might say to the contrary.

The replaceability of targets would seem to make lethal violence all the more plausible. Scores of dealers ply their trade on a daily basis, providing a readily available and abundantly substitutable supply of victims. Contraband, moreover, can be seized whether or not they comply—something not necessarily true in other high-magnitude heists. Bank robberies, for example, typically require victim assistance to deactivate security codes and open safes (see Luckenbill 1980). At the time of the offense, drug robbers typically are angry, desperate, inebriated, and under pressure to make something happen. They are volatile people anyway, with a paranoid style of attribution and a decided inability to be empathic (see Dodge and Newman 1981; Toch 1969; Wright and Decker 1997). The presence of accomplices (not wholly uncommon) only amplifies their predisposition to lash out; there is an audience to impress and thus added reinforcement for violence (see Felson 1982; Zimbardo 1970). Pressing needs and murky judgment make for a combustible mix; disinhibitors to lethal aggression evaporate—particularly when rewards are highly valued and perceptibly imminent (see Hull 1981; Steele and Southwick 1985).

That lethal violence appears neither common nor preferred (at least, according to the drug robbers' reports) is therefore instructive. It suggests that their contingent threats may be up to task. Staring down the barrel of a loaded gun can make even large amounts of drugs and money rapidly lose their intrinsic value for victims otherwise bent on recalcitrance. Robbery is recognized to be what it rightly is—a cost of doing business in a high-risk world, an occupational hazard that must be tolerated with equanimity (Wright and Decker 1997). As long as sellers can posture later in ways that make losses look petty or unconcerning, damage to their reputations need not be permanent. And financial losses can almost always be recovered, though admittedly, with variable difficulty. Retaliation will come later, after victims have had the opportunity to mull over the incident and ponder an appropriate course of action. Revenge, as they say, is a dish best eaten cold. Drug robbers must respond to this threat, as Chapter 5 will attest.

NOTES

1. Operating at night / wearing disguises provided the additional benefit of identity concealment, critical given the risk of retaliation. Two exceptions (times when this wasn't important) involved robberies motivated by revenge (in which offenders generally want victims to know who's robbing them) and those triggered by opportunity (in which offenders may not have a mask available when a suitable target emerges).
2. The same could be said of robberies that suddenly cropped up while in the presence of others, given the ease and rapidity with which rewards could be secured.
3. Such threats have a longer-term purpose as well, by enticing victims to think twice about seeking payback. Lasting fear withers the drive for retaliation.
4. Though this happened inside a dwelling, the example is provided to illustrate the general theme.
5. The foregoing data presentation is not intended to suggest that the drug robbers are always in control and are always successful. However, the data collection techniques used here are biased toward completed offenses.

Managing Retaliation

ILLICIT DRUG MARKETS represent a context in which law is unavailable as a matter of course. The absence of legal redress is a defining characteristic of all underworld enterprise. Those who violate the law cannot be "victims" and as such, lose the privilege of juridical protection. If and when grievances arise, they must be resolved informally. Retaliation emerges as the modal response.

Referred to variously as secret social control, crime as self-help, or coercive unilateral social control (Black 1983; Horwitz 1990), retaliation denotes an act of harm inflicted on another in return for being wronged oneself. At its heart, retaliation is compensatory action designed to correct a perceived inequity. "Its hallmark is balance" (Black 1993:91) and as such, the behavior is grounded conceptually in the norm of reciprocity. This norm holds that persons will respond "to others in ways and to the degree that resembles that of the other person's initial [action]" (Craig 1999:141; Gouldner 1960). The greater the perceived imbalance, the more likely retaliatory responses become. In marginal contexts where normative support for violence already is strong, the desire for payback will be especially powerful (see also Barreca 1995; Horwitz 1990; Marongiu and Newman 1987).

Failure to avenge drug robberies can have grave long-term consequences. Insofar as fleeced sellers must answer to someone else for lost cash and drugs, the consequences of capitulation will be grim: The wrath of higher-level suppliers is swift and severe, and to chance it is unwise (see Johnson et al. 1985; Maher 1997:91–92). As one long-time drug seller remarked, "Got to realize man, most dudes in the city, man, they selling for somebody else out of town. . . . [If they get ripped off,] he's [supplier's] in the rear also too. . . . He got to find me to make up." The reputational damage borne from surrender is equally germane. On the streets, respect is the "coin of the social order" (Anderson 1999:33). To submit without evening the score is to squander it. For many, this can be a "fate worse than death." The chronic exploitation likely to follow makes life only more unbearable (Anderson 1999:33, 37, 88, 97; see also Black 1983).

The importance of (1) selecting targets that are perceptually soft, easily intimidated, interpersonally unfamiliar, and geographically distant; (2) concealing identities through the use of masks, darkness, and camouflage; and (3) plundering satisficing rather than rapacious amounts, already has been established. Such strategies may be useful for shaping the "supply side" of retribution, but they are inherently limited. The effects of intimidation can wear off. Soft targets might enlist the services of a hit man. Small quantities of contraband can appear large to the person from whom they are pilfered. Word of a drug robber's identity or whereabouts can leak. Anonymity might be breached by the most innocuous of chance encounters. The more recent a robbery, the more troublesome run-ins can become: Victims' memories are fresh, their sensitivity to interpersonal cues keen, and their thirst for revenge acute. Even with a disguise, cues such as tattoos, jewelry, voice, demeanor, gait, size, and height remain tell-tale signs for especially attentive victims. Masks draw only more attention to them during the robbery: essentially, they are the only things to attend to.

Drug robbers had to manage their post-offense behavior accordingly. First and foremost, they could not leak information, either through actions or words, that might expose their recent misdeeds. Flashing the spoils from a freshly committed robbery—

cash, expensive clothing, jewelry—was a sure-fire way to identify oneself as a "player" who needed to be a taught a lesson. Showing off items that could be traced directly back to a specific victim was worse still. Both actions constitute dangerous proclamations of one's dirty work—public affronts that cannot go unpunished (Wright and Decker 1997). Spanky seemed to recognize this pro-actively—refusing to seize an expensive necklace from a prior victim for fear it would ultimately identify him:

> I didn't want no chain 'cause the kind of chain he got, he had like a fat herringbone with a dagger on it and everybody know that's Tyrell's[2] chain. [Tyrell] seen with a size herring-bone that big and if anybody else have it [others] would know it was his and they probably would have got hurt.

Since stolen items typically were fenced [sold] quickly after the offense, or displayed only in "safe" venues, the real exposure concern was talk. On the streets, there is no such thing as discussing a drug robbery in confidence. One never knows when, where, or to whom a story might be repeated. Word travels fast and everybody is into everybody else's business. Though bragging may be functional for enhancing one's reputation, the risk of exposure is a prohibitive price to pay. Post-offense silence thus became the order of the day:

> It don't make no sense to brag about it because, see, you could be bragging and ain't no telling this [person] might be somebody's cousin or relative, anybody, you see what I'm saying? So therefore you say to yourself, why start bragging about shit? I'm not gonna get a bunch of motherfuckers here, "I robbed this bitch you dig, and this, you dig," and just see what happened. Her cousin might be there, anybody's sister, brother, any motherfucker.— *June Bug*

Ray Dog agreed, remarking that "You don't go around telling every motherfucker that you [did] that. That's how you get yourself killed." Or, as Buck observed, "Why would I tell on myself? . . . I go to two or three [offender] funerals every year. . . . I don't want to get shot." Lewis, Slim, and Low Down concluded similarly:

> You don't put your goodies out in the street to everybody. . . . Everybody business ain't everybody business, you know. . . . Just keep it to yourself, then won't nobody know what you did. Only thing he can say, "Damn, somebody robbed me last night, man!" That's it.

> There's nothing to brag about. See, that's information. You don't brag about what you do. . . . Why would I tell these peoples about my business, what I'm doing? . . . Now, if somebody else come up to them and tell them, "Damn, you know, your partner robbed me last night." He'll know for his self. But telling that there (inaudible), "I knocked this fellow off last night for about $600, $700, $800 and 15, 16 rocks," you know. Why would I brag to you about that there?

> I don't brag about it 'cause too many people talk too much. . . . Nine times out of ten if I keep saying [how I robbed some dealer], [some] dude probably be like, "Man, some [guy] robbed me, I don't even know who it is." "Oh man," [another person will say], I know who it is." . . . "Man, tell me who it is." Stuff like that happens. . . . He'll probably say, "I'll kill your ass; I'm gonna get you." . . . You just got to be real careful.

Loose talk also risked having a price put on one's head—a very real threat in the snitch-infested world of the streets. To down-and-out drug users, even small offers of money or drugs can serve as powerful enticements to tattle. "Crack dealers . . . will pay a crackhead to tell [them], you know, where this person [drug robber] at," Baby Doll revealed. "You don't let anybody know what you're doing." Three Eyes agreed: "[You tell and] the next person get jealous or get mad at you, turn you into the dope dealer for some money just for the information."

The importance of post-offense silence was rivaled only by the need for hypervigilance—the near obsessive attention to one's surroundings and the behavior of others. Recall that drug robbers and their victims inhabit the same general social world. Potential danger lurks around every corner, and no situation—no matter how innocuous it may seem—is immune from retaliatory significance (see Katz 1988:221). Vulnerability varies directly with insouciance, so it was crucial that drug robbers monitor their interpersonal field. Many reportedly assessed their surroundings and the behavior of others with a zeal that bordered on fixation:

> You got to watch. I mean you could be inside some store, anybody walking behind you, you got to be like this here, man. You got to look around corners, you got to look around everywhere, you see what I'm saying? I mean, even when I go to my mom's house sometimes, I got to walk around through the back, go around to the backyard, look around in the yard, see if anybody back there. . . . You stop coming outside during the day, you come out at night-time . . . because during the day they notice you during the day. See, at night it's dark. They might see you in a car or something. Then you change a lot. . . . You got to change your whole personality towards a lot of things. You got to change your attitude.
> —*Ray Dog*

> You got to be cautious, man. It's a job, man, all day long wherever you be at, looking behind you. 'Cause one day, man, some motherfucker gonna get me. . . . You take $100,000 from a person, take it from him, you think he forget? Don't get me wrong. If they caught me tripping, man, I don't be here. If they was able to find out where they could actually get me or where I lay my head at night, I wouldn't be worth a goddamn dime.—*Curly*

Though such behavior might appear paranoid to the typical middle-class observer, to drug robbers it made perfect sense. Retaliation has a long half-life. Chance encounters are always a possibility, and dire consequences await those who let their guard down. Lying low and altering one's regular behavior patterns became not only logical, but essential:

> I normally go into a shell [after a robbery] . . . weeks at a time. I do a lot of cooking, cleaning. . . . I'm paranoid. . . . I mean, I'll go to the grocery store, I might go to a movie way out in Chesterfield [a suburb in St. Louis county] somewhere. . . . I might go to Kansas City and shop for some clothes. . . . I don't venture out much. I change cars every six months. . . . You never know [when someone's going to come back at you], you never know.—*Buck*

Most drug robbers insisted that attending to their environment could never really be suspended. As the frequency and magnitude of their offenses increased, the need for sustained vigilance rose. "The more you rob," Do-dirty expounded, "you always gonna run into [victims] because St. Louis is too small. You bound to run into him. Ain't no place you hide in the city of St. Louis at all." "I see a lot of people that I done shit to," Darnell added. "I mean I laugh on the inside [but] I always keep my eyes open. My uncle told me, 'You know you've done a lot of wrong to these guys. Now that you're getting your life together [getting off heroin], you really got to keep your head up. 'Cause there is a time when all this shit might come back on you and when you are ready to face it, then face it.'" YoYo claimed that such prospects tempered the very attractiveness of drug robbery:

> [You] be taking a chance with your life everyday. . . . I mean, you walking around looking behind your back at every turn, every move you make, it ain't that easy, it's not that easy. [Drug robbery] sounds good, the money sounds good but it ain't that easy and that's the God honest truth, it's really not that easy. When you do dirt, you got to watch your back at all times 'cause you never know if somebody gonna get you. . . . One day you can reap what you sow, you reap what you sow.

Decisions about whether, when, or how to return to the actual offense site and contiguous areas underscored the extent to which
hypervigilance constrained the drug robbers' post-offense movement patterns. Most steered clear of these locations for several
weeks to several months. "You give it three or four months before
you roll back through there," Do-dirty insisted. "And even then,
you don't be riding in your car. . . . [Dude might see you and] he
might tell his partner, 'Man, that's the dude that robbed me' . . .
'That's the dude that got you?' And his partners come around the
corner with a pistol and when you look up, they gonna hit you."
Blackwell claimed to wait a "good four months" before return-
ing. By then, he argued, "they probably ain't worried about it."
Baby Doll declared that she might never be able to go back to an
area in which she had done a drug robbery. Paradoxically, she recognized that her crack habit was so powerful that she might *have*
to go back:

> If I can't find no drugs in the area where I'm hanging out,
> shit, I say, "Oh well," I got to creep over this way [to a set
> where she had robbed]. I got to do a little creeping, you
> know. . . . I'll take a chance.

Indeed, knowing that one had to "watch out" was not always sufficient to inspire evasive conduct. Given the drug robbers' street-
focused lifestyle and frequent consumption of hard psychoactive
drugs, their decision-making abilities often were less than sharp.
And blunted judgment is not conducive to discreet behavior.
Baby Doll recounted a revenge robbery in which she targeted a
dealer who had raped her a few months previously. The dealer-
victim sought immediate retaliation, but was not successful. "He
rolled around looking for us [that night]," she recalled, "and he
went and got, I guess, a couple of his partners and stuff and they
was on the streets. Shit, I had to stay off the street at least about a
good month, at least around in that area, you know." Apparently, however, she went back too early—a decision no doubt influ-
enced by her drug-induced state of intoxication:

> There was one particular time, I was high, tripping, I was
> coming down Sarah [Street]. I didn't even think about it [the
> prospect of retaliation], you know, when you're high you
> forget about these things. [Her previous victim] pulled over
> and he had his little partner with him. . . . He jumped out of
> the car, his friend jumped out. I just took off running. I was
> running, I was running, running for dear life. . . . So one of
> them was riding around and the other one was on foot. So
> then his friend, they couldn't find me, you know. . . . I hid
> down in this vacant building in the basement, you know, un-
> derneath the steps. . . . I don't know, something just saved me
> but he didn't catch me. . . . I waited there and it came to me,
> I said, I knew it [the drug robbery] would come back on me.

The task of hypervigilance was complicated by the drug robbers'
nomadic ways. Most claimed to never "lay their heads" in one
place or area for long, "staying" with kin, friends, girlfriends, and
associates in small intervals of time (see Fleisher 1995:63 for the
semantic distinction between "stay" and "live"). "I'm a floater,"
Slim illustrates. "I can't believe in just sitting there and letting
roots grow up under my feet. I like to move, I like to stay on the
go" (see also Maher 1997:41 on "couch people"). In one sense, the
offenders' free-ranging lifestyles gave them a better chance at
avoiding payback. Mobility allowed them to avoid "hot" areas
(for example, places where they had committed drug robberies)
and provided greater access to hiding places. To be mobile is to
be elusive in a context where evasiveness is critical to avoiding
retaliation.

Yet mobility carried significant risks of its own. In particular, it
increased the odds of chance encounters. The streets are an "en-
capsulated social world" that interweaves participants in an "expansive web of diffuse relations" (Jacobs 1999b:568). Degrees of
separation are few; "almost every element of the network is
somehow 'close' to almost every other element, even those that
are perceived as likely to be far away" (Watts 1999:495). Weak ties
predominate and permit substantial bridging between otherwise
discrete social networks (Granovetter 1973). Isomorphic lifestyles
bring offenders and victims together (Lauritsen et al. 1991). The

more members of a network there are, and the denser that network is, the more likely run-ins become. The principle of "homogamy" predicts that offenders will be the modal *victim* group when they move in areas that contain a disproportionate share of others like them (Lauritsen et al. 1991:267–77; see also Hindelang et al. 1978:256–57). Bus stops, mini-malls, grocery stores, bars, movie theaters, and fast-food restaurants therefore emerge as contexts fraught with risk.

Lady Bug thus described running into a past victim at a local White Castle (fast-food restaurant). She had disguised herself during the offense, so was able to make a narrow escape. "This . . . dude ran up on me," she recounted, "pulled a gun, he was like, 'I remember you!' [You robbed me!]. I said, 'You don't even know me. What's up?' 'Oh, I'm sorry,' [he said], 'I thought you was this other gal.' No, I don't trip off these little punk-ass niggers." Smoke Dog neglected to cover his face during a previous drug robbery, with near-disastrous consequences later. "Dude . . . rolled down the city, started shooting at me and I started shooting back, me and my little partner. Started shooting back." These gun battles apparently continued well after the robbery. "We was going to war," Smoke Dog declared. "Every time I see him he shoot at me, it's like that, we shoot at each other." The "war" stopped only when Smoke Dog's antagonist left town, which, of course, he claimed credit for. "I guess he got scared or whatever. . . . I broke him."

One important and widespread response to the threat of such encounters was to carry a firearm at all times. Ever-present but unpredictable risks require a constant state of readiness; surprise attacks can be neutralized only if one is fully prepared (see Wright and Rossi 1986). As Curly insisted, "Never get caught without [your gun], never. When I get out of the car I got it, man, I don't get out of the car without it. Even if I'm getting out of the car to socialize, man, I got it, man." Smoke Dog agreed, proclaiming that "I always have big magnum [.44] with me. Big magnum is always with me. . . . I ride dirty every day, every day, got to. . . . I'm strapped up, believe me, I'm strapped up. . . . That big magnum gonna get busy. That's a quick loader too, he gonna get busy." Ray Dog was more emphatic, insisting that "You got to sleep with

your pistol, you got to eat with your pistol, you got to go to the
bathroom with your pistol, you got to take a shower with your
pistol. . . . Everywhere you go, you got to take your guns with
you."

Bolstered by the confidence that only an ever-present firearm
can provide, most offenders believed they could handle anything
that came their way:

> I'm the type of dude that, when you coming at me, I'm go-
> ing back at you, you know. . . . I done put a lot of people to
> sleep . . . so hey, I ain't no joke. I'll tear a new hole in his ass
> just as quick as I'll tear one in any of these motherfuckers out
> here.—*Ray Dog*

> Come with a gun. Come with your army . . . 'cause it gonna
> take an army to take me down. . . . You gonna kill me or I'm
> gonna kill you. . . . I come to a fight with a big old .45 because
> . . . when they see that big old .45 with a nine-inch barrel on
> here, they bags up, they bags up.—*Do-dirty*

Offenders with violent kin and friends were emboldened further
by the knowledge that, even if they could not handle a particular
situation, the slack would be taken up by others:

> I got seven brothers, seven brothers and thirteen youngsters,
> all of them straight up trigger-finger crazy. . . . Anything that
> happen to me, anything that goes down, I tell them where
> everything is, tell them where this is, this person did it. . . .
> That's a war, you know, that's a straight-up war.—*Ray Dog*

> My little partners and them [get] down and dirty. . . . We're
> talking about hurt dudes.—*Smoke Dog*

> If anybody come tripping . . . they [my partners] already
> know what's up. . . . They got my back. . . . If I have any sta-
> tic, if any motherfuckers act like they gonna do something to
> me, [they get] trigger happy.—*YoYo*

To some extent, comments such as these strain credulity. Street offenders hold each other in low esteem and relationships among them—even those who call each other "partner"—hinge on mutual distrust. Solidarity in the traditional sense of the term barely exists; remember, bonds in this world are premised on a dog-eat-dog mentality (Dunlap 1991). Would-be avengers might talk big, but over time nothing really happens (see Anderson 1999:139). It makes no economic or practical sense to face death or prison to protect those with whom one only is marginally tied (Fleisher 1998:56). Though some drug robbers seemed to recognize this, many continued to hold onto the belief that they somehow would be "covered" in the event of reprisal. Talk of protection may provide all the reassurance necessary. Security comes in saying the words (cf. Fleisher 1995).

In the final analysis, offenders could never really be sure how effectively their retaliatory threat management strategies would work, or if they would work at all. The streets are too chaotic and unpredictable to eradicate the specter of payback. Most resigned themselves to the notion that if retaliation was in their fate, they were powerless to do anything about it. Smoke Dog thus declared that lethal reprisal was "not something I even worry about. . . . I just ain't worried. . . . Forget it." Ladybug claimed that she "ain't scared to die. . . . If they gonna kill me they gonna kill me, [but] you better knock me hard." Baby Doll added that sometimes she thinks about it, but was ultimately going to accept what was in her destiny. "Fuck it, this [drug robbery] is what I do. Whatever happens, happens. That's how you got to look at it." "I got to die from something," J Rock continued. "You [author] could die from eating a piece of meat. The gum you [chewing], you could die of that." Do-dirty and K-red intellectualized in a similar fashion. "I might go home at night and go to sleep and might not even wake up," revealed the former. "If God call me, he call me." "They can kill me, but," K-red continued, "but we all gonna die. We all gonna die pretty soon. . . . We don't stay on earth forever." Though Ray Dog recognized that if his time was up it was up, his self-perceived invincibility convinced him that he could rise up Phoenix-like and do more reprising himself:

If he got me, he got me. I already got it put in my mind like that, man; I ain't fear no death, man, see what I'm saying? I don't fear death, I don't fear dying or nothing, you dig? That would be just caught me with my pants down. He just caught me with my pants down. Best man won, that's all, best man won. He got me because, hey, if I run up over there and he talking that [shit] I'll get him again. I'll put it down on him again.

Fatalistic attitudes are enormously liberating for those with so much to fear. They permit those who express them to shift responsibility for their destiny onto forces over which they have no control. Life is short and "what will be will be," so why obsess about *potential* consequences over which one has no jurisdiction? (Anderson 1999:136–37; see Miller 1958). Such a stance is profoundly empowering as well. Insofar as an "I don't care" mentality makes drug robbers better able to project fearlessness and "true nerve"—both during offenses and long after—their reputation as badasses will be enhanced (Anderson 1999). Would-be antagonists are more likely to recognize that "messing with" such persons is an action that they undertake at prohibitive peril (see Katz 1988). Inasmuch as retaliation is subsequently inhibited, drug robbers enjoy an added measure of protection.

DISCUSSION

Criminologists have long focused on how the threat of sanctions influences the behavior of would-be criminals (for example, Beccaria 1764 [1963]; Bentham 1789 [1973]). "Informal" sanction threats also have attracted considerable attention, with particular emphasis placed on the role of shame and embarrassment (Blackwell et al. 1994; Grasmick and Bursik 1990; Grasmick et al. 1993; Paternoster and Simpson 1996). Initially attractive deviant actions, it is said, become decidedly less appealing when such conscience-linked variables are factored into the decision-making process. Some scholars have gone so far as to suggest that the extralegal consequences of offending may be the "real deterrent and that formal punishment is important only insofar as it triggers informal sanctions" (Bishop 1984:405; see also Gibbs 1989; Paternoster and Iovanni 1986:769; Tittle 1980:241; Williams 1985:148).

Absent from the analysis is an examination of the ways in which the risk of victim retaliation—arguably the ultimate informal sanction—mediates offender decision making. Like shame / embarrassment, retaliation is an outcome of both extralegal and moralistic character. Unlike its brethren, retaliation is unique in its ability to operate exclusively of formal sanctions. Shame and embarrassment, by contrast, tend to be triggered only after legal sanctions arise. As such, retaliation is capable of deterrence in its own right; to be sure, it may be the sole sanction offenders face. Shame and embarrassment, moreover, have a middle-class bias that retaliation typically lacks. As affective responses, they tend to influence only those with substantial stakes in conformity. Offenders in general, and drug robbers in particular, often lack such stakes and therefore the "ability" to experience much of either emotion (see, for example, Tittle 1980).

The potential for retaliation exists in every crime, though some offenses—like drug robbery—clearly are more conducive to it than others. The tactics designed to manage this threat are not unike "restrictively deterrent" behaviors offenders use to evade *formal* sanction threats. The only difference lies in the intended target (other offenders rather than the police). Perhaps this is because retaliation as social control more resembles a formal sanction—in its degree of threatened physical incapacitation, permanence, and external sourcing—than an informal one. Shame and guilt, by contrast, are *emotions* that deter *indigenously*.[3]

Though the process of retaliation management may give the appearance of compartmentalized behavior, it probably is not so clear-cut. Some tactics will be used in degrees, in specific sequences, in concert, or in lieu of others. Others will serve as backstops for strategies that are not up to task. The weakest of within-offense intimidation attempts, for example, can be "covered" later by many of the remedial measures explored in this chapter. If anonymity maintenance fails, hypervigilance offers a countermeasure. Identity leakage is not nearly so damning if one can muster enough firepower to neutralize emergent threats, or can avoid those one has robbed. It is plausible that over time, retaliatory threat-management tactics might even be suspended altogether or, at least, applied with less priority. Bolstered by past success, offenders may believe themselves to be safe from attack. People in general believe they are unlikely to experience negative events (Weinstein 1980; see also Horswill and McKenna 1999), and this belief is especially strong among street criminals.[4] High-risk situations are redefined as normal or routine (Lejeune 1977:130; see also Paternoster and Piquero 1995 on direct experiences with punishment avoidance). Ultimately, this may cause targets to be selected with less discretion, offenses to be enacted with less precision, or hypervigilance to be exercised with less urgency. Fatalism coupled with heavy drinking, hard-drug use, and fiscal desperation only amplify these tendencies (see also Shover 1996). Given that the risk of retaliation accumulates across offenses, managing retribution may *subjectively* appear less necessary even as it becomes *objectively* more important.

Even if strictly adhered to, the tactics described in this chapter clearly are not foolproof. Some have a real potential for creating the opposite of their intended effect. Weapons, for instance, provide protection but can entice their carriers to (1) lay low for shorter periods of time, (2) travel to areas that otherwise would be considered off-limits, or (3) be less vigilant. Moving around in "strange" areas ensures greater anonymity but may confound a quick getaway in the event it becomes required (assuming escape routes are less known). Enlisting others to watch one's back engenders security but exposes one to the hazards of gossip (particularly given the precarious loyalty and shifting alliances of the streets). Hypervigilance is functional but also is emotionally draining. Ultimately, it may be suspended altogether in favor of a fatalistic, "fuck it" mentality (Walters 1990) that emboldens offenders to commit even more crimes, or leads them to dismiss the importance of retaliatory threat management in favor of preemptive incapacitation. (For an analogy, see Sherman 1993 on the "defiance effect;" see also Brown et al. 1996 on the psychic costs of offending.) Both function to increase the offenders' aggregate risk.

Undeniably, the retaliatory threat management tactics described here have generic importance outside the realm of drug robbery. They are part and parcel of a more general calculus reflected in all forms of victimizing behavior. Discretion and hypervigilance, for example, are analogous to the behavior of any prudent bank robber or street mugger seeking to elude those who might seek them out. So are weapons carrying, mobility, and the enlistment of friends as "lookouts."[5] The difference is that law-abiding victims, almost by definition, are unlikely to retaliate. Typically, they lack the knowledge, skill, and disposition to do so, as well as the moral conviction to take the law into their own hands (and thus break it). Formal justice exists to shoulder their burden. Fortunately for would-be offenders, the same tactics that discourage retaliation may also reduce the victim's willingness to seek official redress.

The point is that law cannot be useful if it is unavailable. Black-market enterprise by no means monopolizes this condition; analogous instances exist aplenty in the wider society. War, civil unrest, and natural catastrophes periodically threaten a return to the Hobbesian state of nature, where informal social control is the only kind available (see Black 1983), or law might be present but not granted legitimacy—such as when police are perceived to be an occupying force, or when formal authority is judged to be capricious, random, and inequitable (see Anderson 1999; Sherman 1993). Law might be present but not "usable"—perhaps because of status differences or social distance between complainants and offenders (Horwitz 1990). Law also can be unavailable because it is ineffectual. We know that the vast majority of offenses go undetected or unacted upon by police. Temporal gaps between detection, arrest, and conviction undermine the celerity of punishment. Bungled prosecutions sometimes result in the guilty going free. As confidence in the system wanes and skepticism rises, the perceived need to take matters into one's own hands increases. Retaliation becomes the only way to bring the swiftness, certainty, and severity of punishment back into deterrence.

Recent legislative initiatives—harsh prison terms for minor offenses, mandatory minimum sentences, cries for corporal punishment (i.e., Singapore-style), and the reinvigoration of capital punishment—testify to a widespread perception that formal crime-control mechanisms are too weak and need to be enhanced. Indeed, many state legislatures have gone so far as to allow ordinary citizens to carry concealed weapons, a policy with the ironic, if unintended, consequence of extending the retaliatory potential of criminal victims to law-abiding citizens. Behind such measures lies the notion that the threat of retaliation is a powerful deterrent. In this sense, CCW laws may represent an attempt to formalize informal deterrence.

It remains hard to believe, however, that victims of *drug robbery*—in the face of tactics designed to thwart retaliation—will summarily shrug their shoulders and move on. If unilateral submission is the untenable proposition so many scholars make it out to be, how the wrong gets "righted" becomes the issue. We know that violence tends to be exchanged reciprocally (Singer 1986:61). We also know that the motive behind such exchanges is often moralistic or normative in nature—a kind of "you got me so I have to get you back" mentality (see Black 1983). If the tactics described in this chapter and elsewhere work as effectively as the drug robbers suggest, reciprocal exchanges will be stifled. The better they work, the more unbalanced reciprocity becomes. Unable to exact revenge on those who robbed them and eager to make back losses, victims might be enticed to engage in unfocused retribution—predation displaced onto uninvolved third parties (see also Sherman 1993 on "indirect defiance").

We know that favorable identities can be retrieved whether or not vengeance is direct (Melburg and Tedeschi 1989). Researchers refer to this as redistributive justice, wherein aggrieved parties restore equity by harming someone other than those responsible for the original injustice ("any member of a particular category [can] be held responsible for the blameworthy action of another member.") (Tedeschi and Felson 1994:366; see also p. 246). The crime-saturated drug sets in which predatory offenses such as drug robbery are performed provide testimony to its potential. Such areas have a readily available group of would-be victims in a discrete space whose lifestyle patterns render them easy and logical targets (see Lauritsen et al. 1991). This creates ideal conditions for violence to spiral beyond any given victim-offender dyad.

The extent to which this dynamic played into the historic levels of systemic instability and violence generated between 1984 and 1991—a major contemporary controversy in criminology—remains open to question. Though the emergence of crack cocaine seems to be the primary cause (Blumstein and Rosenfeld 1998), unfocused "retribution" resulting from drug robberies may well have had a concomitant effect on the diffusion process. The threat of retaliation motivates widespread arming. Guns are acquired by individuals peripherally involved in the conflict. Weapons are used in an increasingly casual manner (see Blumstein and Rosenfeld 1998). The ironic consequence is that, while retaliatory threat management tactics are geared toward impeding violence against drug robbers at the individual level, their implementation may create more violence on a systemic level.

Even if we accept the notion that retaliation is more successful than not and that predation is indeed *directly* reciprocal, cycles of violence do not necessarily become less problematic. Retaliation can very well lead to counter-retaliation, which in turn can spawn even more violence as increasing numbers of tangentially associated individuals get drawn in to budding conflicts (see Goldstein 1985). Given that formal social control on the streets is so lacking in effectiveness, credibility, and deterrent value (see, for example, Paternoster 1987; Paternoster and Piquero 1995; Sherman 1993), such diffusion is only to be expected. Indeed, street justice—once the modal form of dispute resolution—may be especially strong in this vestigial context because police often perceive such venues to be undeserving of formal intervention (see Klinger 1997). The more unstable the context, the more entrenched informal justice becomes, and the more likely formal authorities will "look the other way." This, in turn, engenders even greater instability, triggering a self-enclosed cycle of reinforcing behavior (cf. Lemert 1953). Whether such chaos is triggered by the diffusion of violence outward from some central point of origin (for example, the original dealer-victim / drug robber dyad) or from microbursts of violence exploding across random nodes in the street-level microstructure (i.e., unfocused predation) ultimately makes little difference. Undoubtedly, both dynamics are occurring at the same time, creating the tangled web of predation we see in so many high-crime urban locales across the country.

NOTES

1. This chapter was adapted from *Criminology*, 38 (2000):171–98; portions are reprinted here with permission.
2. Tyrell is a pseudonym constructed to protect Spanky from possible exposure.
3. Though embarrassment also is externally imposed, it means nothing unless or until it generates an emotive response within the psyche of the offender.
4. Langer (1975:311) refers to this as the "illusion of control," a phenomenon in which expectancies of "personal success . . . [are] inappropriately higher than the objective analysis would warrant."
5. Thanks go to Bob Bursik and an anonymous referee from the journal *Criminology* for bringing these points to my attention.

CHAPTER SIX

Order Beyond the Law

S OCIAL ORDER — ITS PROBLEMS, prospects, and possibilities in a world beyond the law—is an implicit theme running throughout this book. Early on, it was identified as a core concern. Early on, it also was promised that its broader implications would be explored. Now it is time to make good on that promise.

The quest to explain social order is as old as sociology itself. No system can survive, or survive for long, in its absence. Conventional wisdom holds that order is not possible without cohesion and there can be no cohesion without social control. Social control refers broadly to "all of the human practices and arrangements that contribute to social [stability] and . . . influence people to conform" (Black 1993:4). Social control can be implicit or explicit, individualistic or institutional, informal or formal. Styles of control vary, from repressive and compensatory to conciliatory and therapeutic. The end goal, however, is invariably the same: to neutralize deviance, settle conflict, and restore reciprocity. Social stability depends on the efficient resolution of emergent grievances (see Black 1983; Horwitz 1990; Gouldner 1960).

Law represents social control at its most advanced. Legal systems tend to evolve in complex societies, where diverse, heterogeneous populations require official methods of conflict resolution. An intricate matrix of adjudicators, arbitrators, and mediators develops to absorb disputes that cannot otherwise be settled. Access to the law is widespread and reasonably democratic except, of course, for law violators. Offenders are beyond the law and lose legal protections in times of need. Their disputes must be resolved informally.

For them, street justice becomes the rule of the day. Retaliation is used to right perceived wrongs. Order is predicated on violence and its threat. All encroachments, no matter how minor, must be reprised. Tolerance equals weakness and weakness invites future exploitation. Even if outside authorities were available, they cannot be enlisted. Powerful conduct norms militate against reliance on "the man." Status and security come only by taking care of one's own business (Anderson 1999:307–8). To be labeled a snitch is to lose all hope of respect.

In the outlaw world of the streets, respect is everything. Conventional means of securing it have largely ceased to exist (Wilson 1996). Drastic changes in the post–World War II economy—deindustrialization, the widespread loss of high-paying manufacturing jobs, and the out-migration of social capital—have left vast numbers behind with little opportunity and even less hope. For such unfortunates, respect becomes an "almost external entity" that must be seized, protected, and maintained at all costs. Respect rises by putting others down, so everyone's "public bearing must send the unmistakable, if sometimes subtle, message that one is capable of violence, and possibly mayhem, when the situation requires." (Anderson 1999:37, 72).

The image one projects is not everything, it is the only thing. The streets are theater, a caricature of the larger cinematic society which endorses style over substance (see Denzin 1995). Every encounter is fraught with reputational significance. Demeanor and comportment are vital indicators of one's essential self, but conflicts emerge as the ultimate proving ground. How one reacts under fire provides unobstructed insight into his essential character. Those who pass muster need not worry about future encroachments, nor need they campaign for regard. They gain it rather by the "force of their manner" (Anderson 1999:75). True badasses occupy the apex of street social hierarchies, feared for their exploitive capabilities yet envied for their insularity from exploitation (see Katz 1988).

Obviously, order predicated on violence is inherently tenuous. Disputes have a strong tendency to ignite "conflict spirals" (Lawler 1986), and conflict spirals threaten systemic breakdown (Black 1983; Horwitz 1990:132). Each violent act spawns yet more violence: "Just when one side may regard the score as settled, because in its view the other's suffering matches its own, the other side is likely to see a huge imbalance calling for [predatory] redress" (Baumeister and Campbell 1999:211). Urban drug markets provide testimony to their potential. Though formal social control is not totally absent, its presence can paradoxically make things worse rather than better. On the streets, the police represent an alien force with hostile intentions. They are seen as corrupt and arbitrary. They use discretion for nefarious ends. They are adversaries one wants to avoid—predators with a badge (see also Anderson 1999; Sherman 1993). Their war mentality and pernicious tactics fuel social disorganization and erode informal social controls. This helps to create a "jungle" atmosphere that prompts ordinary people to develop their own brutal brand of vigilantism (Miller 1996:2, 102).

Enforcement strategies only make matters worse. Crackdowns, sweeps, saturation patrol, covert operations, and the like tear up existing crime turf and reshuffle it, which promotes additional chaos (Tidwell 1992). Such tactics also destabilize an already volatile climate—making drug robbery and associated forms of predation more, not less, likely. Permit the following elaboration.

Transactional duration and arrest risk are directly related, so sales must be as speedy as possible. The more rapid the transaction, the more furtive it becomes and the less control one can exert over its outcome. Hurried dealers tend to focus, and this chances critical mistakes. Sellers may handle themselves or their product in less cautious ways, allow buyers to get closer than they should, or give them unjustified latitude with the merchandise (see Jacobs 1999a). Seeking insulation from the police, dealers enhance their vulnerability to predators. Dark, out-of-the-way selling locales permit predators to sneak up undetected and to commit robberies with reduced fear of being seen. Private dwellings, meanwhile, attract a visible flow of customers to a dedicated location, which makes dealers easier to spot and target (see also Jacobs and Miller 1998). Selling off a beeper may offer greater insularity at first, but regular patterns will soon be discernible. Mobile dealers are especially unlikely to tote weapons (for fear of arrest), enhancing their susceptibility further still.

Insofar as the risk of arrest compels sellers to retreat to their own transactional circles, unfamiliar but needy users will require middlemen. Hard-core street addicts known to dealers and sufficiently "trusted" by would-be purchasers typically step in to perform this service (Furst et al. 1999). Such persons, however, are entirely untrustworthy—shorting and ripping off those who employ them (Maher 1997). The same happens after novices fill the distributional vacuum left by stable first-tier vendors removed by arrest (see Maher and Dixon 1999:504; see also Curtis 1993). Burns prompt retaliation and in worlds beyond the law, retaliation ignites counter-retaliation.

Rip-offs and violence obviously are bad for business. Customers who fear getting swindled, or getting sucked into a conflict spiral, are likely to purchase somewhere else, or perhaps not at all. Stagnating demand requires sellers to cultivate new buyers or steal existing ones from other sellers; both require tactics that increase their likely exposure to risk. If sellers opt instead to add more dilutant to their product (another widely used strategy to stabilize profit margins), customers will require more cash to secure the equivalent high. Income-generating crime, the main source of drug revenue, often rises in response. As systemic instability climbs, so will prices—which are enormously risk-sensitive. Higher prices lure new suppliers, elevating competition and worsening systemic violence (at least in the short term, before equilibrating factors come into play; see Riley 1998). If and when violence spills over into nondrug market sectors, lay citizens are more likely to arm themselves for self-protection; persons inevitably react "violently to conditions that violate" (Hamid 1998:172). Routine disputes are more prone to culminate in lethal violence (see Smith and Uchida 1988), cycling back to inspire even more instability.

If we assume that both the absence and presence of law makes things worse rather than better, and that drug-market violence drives urban violence in general, the question of order remains. The effectiveness of the "code of the street" (Anderson 1999) in quelling instability is limited at best. Despite those who believe that the threat of violence—the heart of the code—serves as a "kind of policing mechanism by encouraging people to trust others with a certain respect or . . . face the consequences" (Anderson 1999:105), posturing and display work only for so long. Eventually, one will have to put one's money where one's mouth is. As Gould (1999:376) observes, people may "try to prevent [conflict] by asserting, implicitly or explicitly, that they will act [on their threats, but] the fact is that . . . [they] have to live up to their claims if these claims are to have any [future] value." When words become action, real trouble begins.

Yet how real is this trouble? The street code is ideology; reality is far different. Retaliation may not be as substantial a threat as the code makes it out to be. The majority of street offenders are improvident hedonists who seek short-term pleasure to the exclusion of almost everything else. Tracking down brigands is difficult, time-consuming work with significant opportunity costs. The lack of a retaliatory infrastructure makes reprisal a war that many have neither the resources nor wherewithal to declare. An appreciable fraction may well treat their victimization as a learning experience—one worth the loss if that loss is small, easily replenished, or if future robberies can be prevented as a result. Others might chalk the experience up to "the game," recognizing that those who play with fire inevitably get burned. Still others will diffuse retaliatory responsibility onto unreliable others (for example, hit men), or refrain from reprising out of fear—particularly if they believe that *they* might be reprised first. Retribution is a two-way threat, and victims have an equally great chance of being victimized again if they seek revenge, or so the pursued offenders want them to believe. Ray Dog's story is illustrative. After robbing a dealer of $5,000 in cash, $2,500 in jewelry, and a kilo and a half of cocaine (street value: $30,000 to $60,000), he claimed the victim told him to call off the dispute:

He said leave it alone because of all the spots he hang out at, that was number one. I know where he lives at, I know where he be at, I know what kind of cars he drive, you know, and getting up on him ain't no problem cause he like to go out and party too much so getting up on him ain't no problem. I can meet him inside a tavern real quick [and do him before he does me.] . . . Those guys [are] very intimidated of me because, I guess, the lifestyle: I carry and they know. . . . Busting a cat's head wouldn't mean shit.

Even if aggrieved parties run into perpetrators unexpectedly, they may be unarmed, unprepared, or in a setting inappropriate for retaliation. A small number of reprisals thwarted for any number of these reasons can prevent significant instability. Remember, extensive conflict spirals often emerge from singular disputes. As long as one can talk tough, face need not be lost.

DRUG ROBBERY AS SOCIAL CONTROL

The extent to which drug robbery restricts the growth, expansion, or mere existence of drug markets is a matter of considerable interest (see Wright and Decker 1997). Violence is a strong deterrent to drug-market participation—far stronger, more certain, and without a doubt, more swift than the equivalent threat of legal sanctions. Criminologists have indeed recognized that the driving force behind deterrence is informal sanctions (Bishop 1984). The focus, however, has been on internal psychological states—shame and embarrassment in particular (as noted in Chapter 5). The role that *other offenders* play in deterring crime largely has been ignored.

Dealing drugs is attractive because it offers perceptibly high rewards at acceptable risk. But this hedonistic calculus is fluid. Instability can inspire offenders to seek safer, more attractive alternatives. Desistance and displacement inevitably occur when systemic violence gets bad enough. Some dealers will be lured into the legal economy, particularly during periods of rapid expansion. Others will switch to nonviolent property crime. More will do both; the line between legal and illegal work is not a sharp one, as offenders "double up" on income sources or transition between the two (Freeman 1996:14, 16). If displacement into property crime is sufficiently widespread, surpluses in stolen goods will induce downward price pressures on merchandise bartered for drugs, which ultimately suppresses demand. Less money for drugs translates into less time in risky places among volatile people, and less opportunity for violence to feed off property crimes—unintended, but real, benefits (see Felson 1997; also Jacobs 1999a:126). Of course, the attraction of seizing cash and drugs will likely rise in return, inspiring concomitant increases in (drug) robbery. Insofar as personal and vicarious experience with violence rises as well, desistance and decline among existing market participants will accelerate. Would-be entrants will be increasingly reticent to join the fray.

Though sellers old and new may react by making themselves harder targets, drug robberies now are more likely to become homicides; predators realize the best way to neutralize armed and recalcitrant targets is to use lethal force. Less fearsome adaptations are not necessarily better for drug-market vitality. Carrying smaller amounts of contraband on one's person (to lower the odds of high-magnitude heists), decreasing the quality of the product one sells, or reducing one's accessibility to customers each can diminish it: Demand and search time are inversely correlated; use goes down when drug buying becomes a hassle (see Moore 1977). Extended search time also translates into heightened exposure to formal sanction risks, raising the odds of customer incapacitation (many of whom have outstanding arrest warrants). If purchase attempts become more frequent (because bulk quantities are less available), aggregate risks of incapacitation will climb further still (Hamid 1998:107). Would-be buyers will find it increasingly difficult to secure small, reliable, and inexpensive quantities—siphoning off a potential source of future demand (see, for example, Reuter and Kleiman 1986). Since users often become dealers (to finance their consumption), fewer users ultimately mean fewer dealers—introducing greater upward price pressures on retail quantities. The smaller the market, the more susceptible it becomes to formal social control (Rengert 1996); even the best protected and most sophisticated distributors cannot stay insulated for long (Hamid 1998:105). Wholesale drug market implosion may be a tipping point away.

Though possible, all of this is speculation and ignores the fact that drug-market organization is not static. Distributors migrate to safer areas. They become less visible and more insular. They retreat and come back when stability returns. They become more organized as well. As a precondition for survival, freelancers form loose confederations and, ultimately, "vertical business" operations characterized by pooled interdependence, hierarchical differentiation, and well-defined employer–employee relationships (see Johnson et al. 1992). Labor is broken down into more precise duties. Runners, steerers, holders, stashers, lookouts, and enforcers perform functions once enacted by solitary individuals. With organization comes control, and with control comes stability. Increasingly, participants find methods to settle disputes that need not involve lethal aggression (Blumstein 1995:12). Transactional security rises. Markets reattain equilibrium. The flow of lost demand is stanched. "Professionalized" distribution may cause markets to endure longer and in more meaningful forms than they otherwise would (see Dorn and South 1990).

But *this* speculation ignores the cultural ethos of the street corner, an ethos that renders subservience of any kind unacceptable. Resentment of authority and external control is a hallmark trait for those seeking to avoid emotional confinement at all costs (see Fleisher 1998:145). Freedom from subordination and the ability to do what one wants, when one wants to do it, are essential for those whose lives are defined by marginalization (Jacobs 1999a). Yes, drug selling is profitable, entry is easy, and opportunities are abundant (Akerstrom 1985), but the real allure of "slinging" is autonomy (Bourgois 1995). Dealers can work as little or as much as they want. There are no preassigned duties. There is no boss to answer to. The only obligations one must meet are those one sets, and even these are not requisite. Rewards can be disposed of in whatever fashion one wishes. And selling drugs provides a sense of personal mastery and accomplishment available in few other realistically available vocations. Vertically organized business models threaten all of this, empowering structures at the expense of individual agency. Interdependence may enhance security but at a prohibitive cost for those who believe they should never be under anyone else's thumb. (On the role of autonomy in human motivation, see Deci and Ryan 1985.)

Street offenders tend to believe in their own invincibility anyway. This has a powerful tendency to undermine the (perceived) need for protection; "someone's going to 'get got,' it just won't be me," the thinking goes. Even those who recognize their innate vulnerability may not be prepared to do anything about it. A strong sense of fatalism renders the future a matter of luck and for them, no amount of planning or organization will stave off the inevitable (Walters 1990). There is also the question of whether collective organization really is safer. Hierarchical models develop in later evolutionary stages of drug markets, where workers must be recruited from the most desperate ranks of available employees. With precarious loyalty and unchecked greed, such persons are prone to snitching and theft (see Denton and O'Malley 1999). Indeed, the vast majority of police informants are low-level drug users who supplement their income by tattling (see Collison 1995); as double agents, they take every opportunity to skim drugs from their suppliers or run off with the money. The only defense for dealers is "eternal vigilance, paradoxical distrust, and careful assignment" (Denton and O'Malley 1999:525)— pitifully inadequate measures, to say the least. Hierarchization may be a good idea in theory but may produce the opposite of its intended effect in practice (see Miller 1996).

Relying on natural checks and the self-limiting tendencies of drug markets is inherently unsettling for those who believe the only way to establish control is through tough, external measures. The billions of dollars spent on suppression, interdiction, and incarceration attest to the persisting notion that only officialdom can stop the scourge of drugs. But is this notion valid? Thousands upon thousands of drug-market participants have been incapacitated only to be replaced by thousands more. Scores of high-intensity drug trafficking areas have been squashed, only to be supplanted by new ones. Drug markets, as Dorn and Murji (1992:170) note, are very much like a "squishy balloon: apply pressure to them in one place and there will be some diminution of the problem, yet it is likely that the market will balloon out in another place or an adjacent site, involving new and possibly more cautious or sophisticated dealers and perhaps a different range of drugs." Displacement and its consequences are not unlike "throwing water on an oil fire" (Rengert 1996:8). And when markets are sufficiently large, they can absorb formal social control initiatives without suffering any damage: the enforcement risk in completing any one transaction falls as police resources are spread across numerous sites (Rengert 1996:87, 124). Strategies such as going after "Mr. Big"—trying to behead large-scale dealing operations by going after their leaders—don't work either. They result in new, more complex, and more insular leadership structures even more resistant to interdiction (see Hamid 1998; see also DEA 1997; Rengert 1996).

The point is that drug markets and the predatory behavior they spawn decline first and foremost from within; order inevitably emerges not from external pressure but from an equilibrium that obtains internally (Gasset in McWilliams 1996). Crack, whose growing stigma has whisked demand right from beneath it, has proved this convincingly. Declines in consumption and consumption-related violence have occurred, in large measure, independently of governmental support and interference. Rather than capitalizing on these self-moderating tendencies, policy makers continue to institute draconian measures, "beefing up drug squads and incarcerating people at unprecedented rates for increasingly petty ... charges" (Curtis 1999:20). Though such measures may accelerate the process of decline in the short term, in the long run they entrench the culture of opposition that allows drug markets to thrive. As social disorganization worsens, the decoupling of formal and informal social control will likely become irreparable and the predatory street crime this helps to inspire that much more intractable.

Lasting improvement can be achieved only if policymakers harness the power of informal social control and use it synergistically with formal methods. The challenge becomes one of adjusting the "control mix so as to push [illicit] markets in the least undesired direction" (Dorn and South 1990:186). Such a task obviously is easier said than done. Once the control fabric of a community has been destroyed, it becomes extraordinarily difficult to rejuvenate (see Sampson et al. 1997). Deterioration takes on a life of its own, a "centrifugal force" that triggers a vicious cycle of decay, marginalization, and further decay (see Sampson et al. 1999). Joblessness, dependency, and alienation mount exponentially. Frustration and indignation become pervasive. There is little opportunity and even less hope. Neighborhoods become a "stark tableau of pathology and vice." Citizens traverse them in fear and paranoia (Stansell 1982:321; see Rengert 1996:111 on the "bunker mentality"). Street life emerges as the only realistic alternative, street justice the only viable way to handle its vicissitudes.

CRIME BEYOND THE LAW

Drug robbery is the quintessential offense beyond the law, but scholars often underestimate just how much normal crime actually is as well. Most disputes and conflicts never reach the formal justice system (Black 1983). Those that do "are withdrawn or abandoned before coming to a formal resolution" (Horwitz 1990: 99). An equivalent percentage of crimes of all types goes undetected or ignored by official authorities. Some suggest that the risk of arrest may be as low as one in 11,000, though clearly, this varies by the crime type (see Maher and Dixon 1999). What is clear is that apprehension is mostly a function of being at the wrong place at the wrong time.

The police are reactive and rarely around when offenses occur. Their response time is sufficiently slow to thwart meaningful action when they do arrive. And offenders engage in a wide array of tactics to inhibit the ability of authorities to detect them. The more experienced the offender, the more skilled s/he is at doing this (see Jacobs 1996a and b on restrictive deterrence; Weaver and Carroll 1985).

Even if law violators are caught, incarceration is likely to be brief. Prison is even welcomed by some as a respite from the dog-eat-dog world of the streets (Fleisher 1995). For others, jail functions as a crime school, offering enhanced criminal capital and greater knowledge of how to do more crimes better once one gets out. Growing recidivism rates spawn greater police apathy and even lower detection rates in the future: why, police officers say to themselves, should they risk life and limb to catch criminals who will go right back out on the streets, rested, nourished, and with more skills than they had going in? (cf. Bowling 1999:538).

For police to be effective, they must also be called; social control agents typically do not generate their own cases (Horwitz 1990:99). Yet victims often remain silent. Vast numbers of crimes, even index crimes, go unreported for a multitude of reasons (see BJS 1993; Ennis 1967). Some offenses are so angering or humiliating that nothing short of personal vengeance will do. Others lack enough evidence or are too insignificant to justify calling the authorities (see Laub 1997). Still others trigger an intense need for formal intervention that rapidly dissipates. Yet more transpire between people who know one another (see Wolfgang 1958), and it is "a general principle of social life . . . that one should not introduce exterior power into private domains" (Horwitz 1990:104). This proscription rises with the intimacy of disputants (Black 1983). Not surprisingly, self-help is most common in homogeneous cultures where relational distances are short.

Even in advanced societies, however, self-help "flourishes and most of it involves ordinary citizens who seemingly view their conduct as a perfectly legitimate exercise of social control" (Black 1993:36). Though crime victims may be portrayed as "helpless objects of [predatory] intent who have no option" except to alert formal authorities (Ziegenhagen and Brosnan 1985:676), this most assuredly is not the case. Indeed, the bulk of social control is meted out informally, and many of these actions actually are *criminal* in nature. Robbery, murder, theft, arson, vandalism, and even rape are common moralistic responses designed to "right" past wrongs (Black 1983). Such moralism should not be surprising in light of the existing criminal justice system, a system ostensibly based on deterrence yet one whose deterrent power is so weak. Policy makers have attempted an end-run around this problem by ratcheting up the severity of punishments and by extending punishments to previously unsanctioned behavior, but scare tactics intended to legislate conformity are doomed to fail. Certainty of punishment, not severity, is the key and the certainty remains quite low (see Tittle 1980). Uncaught, unpunished violators must be brought to justice; self-help emerges as the most logical, or available, response.

And then, finally, there are the seductions of crime and street life that contribute to persistent offending and may overcome even potent forms of informal and formal social control. Drug robbery has the makings of a perfect crime. Dealers are walking banks. They are accessible, visible, plentiful, and often unarmed. Many are targets of their own making—flossing, bragging, or otherwise calling attention to themselves. Others are identified through gossip or inside information. The urban topography provides numerous staging areas from which to attack them. Robberies also can be melded with purchases, allowing perpetrators to capitalize on the element of surprise. Compliance is secured rapidly and at acceptable risk. Bystanders are reluctant to intervene; on the streets, no one wants to get involved in someone else's troubles. The threat of retaliation is real but can be reduced to tolerable levels. And dealers obviously cannot go to the police to report their victimization.

Not surprisingly, most drug robbers had no plans to stop committing their crimes any time soon. Though some talked about securing big scores and laying off, such talk seemed less than genuine. The scores from drug robbery *are* big. But they are burned almost as rapidly as they are seized. Additional robberies provide a solution, albeit a temporary one. Freshly obtained revenues facilitate further consumption, inspiring a feedback loop in which at least some drug robbers chronically create the conditions that drive them to their next crime (see also Wright and Decker 1994; 1997). Whether these offenders do this deliberately is open to question. The point is moot, as they are under frequent and considerable pressure to generate funds. Drug robbery provides the most "proximate and performable" solution to their problem (Jacobs and Wright 1999; Lofland 1969).

Self-defeating behavior of this sort is remarkable only to the most naive middle-class observer. The streets are a circumscribed

social world that place extraordinary emphasis on sensory stim-
ulation. The pursuit of illicit action takes precedence over everything else. Hedonism is king. Money exists to be burned. There is
no honor in asceticism; delayed pleasure is for chumps. "Rationality and long-range planning [are dismissed] . . . in favor of en-
joying the moment" (Shover and Honaker 1992:283). Living fast
and loose is more than symbolic or dramaturgical, it cuts to the
core of how identities are constructed and perceived. To be hip
and "in," one must prove it on a continuous basis. Those able to
keep the party going move closer to membership in the mythic
"aristocracy of the streets" (Wright and Decker 1997). Those able
to do so at someone else's expense ascend to the loftiest of sta-
tuses, even more so when their victims are other criminals.

It is hard to imagine these offenders could ever be absorbed
meaningfully into the legitimate world. If absorption were going
to occur, it probably would have already done so. Year 2000, and
the seven years preceding it, marked a period of unprecedented
economic growth in the nation's annals (see Stetkiewitz 1998).
America currently enjoys one of the most robust economies in the
history of modern western civilization. Unemployment is at or
near all-time lows (United States Department of Labor 1998). Real
wages are climbing. Inflation remains in check. Positions in the
legal labor market are opening at unparalleled rates. Employers
are suspending previously important eligibility requirements in
favor of filling empty posts. Persons once thought to be un-
employable are being welcomed with hesitant, but necessarily
open, arms (see also Jacobs 1999a).

Yet few of *these* drug robbers were, or had any intentions of,
capitalizing. Jobs, with their requisite subordination, obedience,
responsibility, and gratification delay, are antithetical to everything they stand for. "Misfits in a world that values precise sched-
ules, punctuality, and disciplined subordination to authority,
[street criminals] value the autonomy to structure life and work
as they wish" (Shover 1991:92). It is unlikely that a "job" would
do them much long-term good anyway. Meaningful life change
can occur only after the prudent accumulation of *social capital*—
relationships with persons in positions of power and influence
(for example, employers, teachers, and ministers; see Coleman

1990). "Vertical" relationships (Reingold 1999) don't simply happen. They must be cultivated, often in fits and starts, over periods of time. This requires effort and a good deal of patience (even more so in the presence of chronic structural barriers), attributes in short supply for those accustomed to going with the flow. There is no mileage to be gained by committing to a course of action that is likely to bring tangible, though non-immediate, rewards (see Shover 1996). Status is something to be seized *now*. People exist to be duped and exploited, not courted. Street capital is what counts and nothing else. Intimidation, deception, and violence are tools to secure it. To approach life any other way is to sell out. On the streets, there are few worse fates (see Anderson 1999).

As another possible source of restraint, guilt had long ago ceased to hold any sway over these offenders. "Pangs of conscience" rarely arose and were promptly dismissed when they did (see also Wright and Decker 1994). Drug robbers had a job to do and a lifestyle to maintain and moral concerns surely were not going to get in their way. "I ain't gonna be feeling any bothers," Slim insisted. "When you out there doing your business you can't be putting no feelings [into it]." "I don't have no pain," Ray Dog echoed, "no pain, no shame, no gain, I don't feel no pity." Or as Lil' Player asked rhetorically, "What I'm gonna do something for and then gonna feel [bad] about it?" Most had convinced themselves that their victims were the real bad guys anyway, and thus merited no sympathy. Drug dealers (the claim went) were leeches that sucked the lifeblood from otherwise vibrant individuals and communities; people who do bad things deserve it when bad things happen to them (see Bandura 1999; Feather 1992; Lupfer and Gingrich 1999). Robbing them was justified action, a Robin Hood–like service for the hopeless, downtrodden, and exploited. The fact that drug robbers would turn around and consume or sell the illicit loot for their own pleasure was a hypocrisy they conveniently ignored, however (see also Peterson 1999).

Though a few respondents recognized that drug robbery was not something they could do forever—some had children and wanted to lead more stable lives, others witnessed the slaying of associates which prompted them to recognize their own mortality—most insisted they would continue committing these crimes indefinitely. "I can't be stopped," K-red declared. "Lay me down, kill me, then I be stopped but as long as my heart keep on going, I'll keep on [doing them]." June Bug proclaimed that "There is nothing in the world that would stop me from doing it. I'm gonna do this until the day I die." Smoke Dog pronounced that robbery was in his blood and that he was "always gonna [do it]."

Even if alternatives were available, it is unlikely they would be recognized. Menacing, volatile losers caught in the grips of street life are notorious for one-track thinking. Each successive offense brings only greater encapsulation. The focus on rewards becomes singular; "deactivation" is decreasingly likely (Heckhausen 2000). Caution becomes more and more expendable and deliberation gives way to impulsive action. The specter of resistance and retaliation is increasingly shunted out of mind. Objectively greater risks are taken, even as they are dismissed as "remote and improbable contingencies" (Shover, 1996:102; see also Pirolli and Card 1999:670). The long-term prognosis for these offenders appears anything but healthy.

Policy makers will be hard-pressed to develop viable strategies for dealing with such incorrigibles. Targeted interventions— from intensive counseling to cognitive therapy to behavioral modification—are not likely to be of much value. People cannot be convinced to change because it's in their best interest, because they'll derive long-term benefits, or because it's the "right thing to do." Enduring transformation comes only after the realization that one's life is no longer manageable (and sometimes not even then). This requires sensitivity, awareness, and a willingness to do things differently. Such qualities are painfully scarce for most of the offenders in this sample.

What policy makers really are up against is a lifestyle, as entrenched as it is intractable, forged from a noxious combination of low self-control, desperation, and cultural imperative. Incapacitation may be the only realistic solution, but one likely to last only as long as the jail sentence; hardened further by prison life, offenders are likely to be only worse after they get out. The larger question of how to reintegrate those who have never been integrated in the first place may, in many ways, be unanswerable.

This is not to say that offenders are immune from policies designed to influence their behavior. The robbers interviewed here targeted drug dealers, at least in part, because the authorities had clamped down so systematically on "normal crime." The point may be moot, as a society that refuses to address the underlying cultural and structural forces that give rise to predatory street offending is doomed to perpetuate the conditions that produce future generations of intractable criminals.

Arguably, the only sure way to eradicate drug robbery is to dry up its opportunity structure, either by legalizing drugs (thus wiping out their black-market value) or by converting wholesale to cashless exchange (see Wright and Decker 1997 on the "cashless society"). Neither is likely to happen any time soon. Even if both or either did, the incorrigible inevitably will adapt, finding new and innovative ways to exploit others for material gain. Deviance and social control, as Ryan (1994) notes, are dialectical processes; each side responds to the other in an endless cycle of evolution. Paradoxically, society may unconsciously yearn for drug dealers to remain viable victims; their presence provides an undeniable safety valve for the rest of us. Their functional importance is only likely to increase as law-abiding citizens become harder, less lucrative targets and as the spiral of desperation in which persistent offenders find themselves locked gets tighter and tighter.

References

Adler, Patricia A. 1985. *Wheeling and Dealing.* New York: Columbia University Press.

Agar, Michael. 1973. *Ripping and Running: A Formal Ethnography of Urban Heroin Addicts.* New York: Seminar Press.

Akerstrom, M. 1985. *Crooks and Squares.* New Brunswick: Transaction Books.

Anderson, Elijah. 1999. *Code of the Street.* New York: Norton.

Arkes, Hal R., and Peter Ayton. 1999. "The Sunk Cost and Concorde Effects: Are Humans Less Rational than Lower Animals?" *Psychological Bulletin* 125:591–600.

Ball, John C., John W. Shaffer, and David N. Nurco. 1983. "The Day-to-Day Criminality of Heroin Addicts in Baltimore: A Study in the Continuity of Offense Rates." *Drug and Alcohol Dependence* 12:119–42.

Ball, John C. 1967. "The Reliability and Validity of Interview Data Obtained from 59 Narcotic Drug Addicts." *American Journal of Sociology* 72:650–54.

Bandura, Albert. 1999. "Moral Disengagement in the Perpetuation of Inhumanities." *Personality and Social Psychology Review* 3:193–209.

Baumeister, Roy F., and W. Keith Campbell. 1999. "The Intrinsic Appeal of Evil: Sadism, Sensational Thrills, and Threatened Egotism." *Journal of Personality and Social Psychology Review* 3:210–21.

Barreca, Regina. 1995. *Sweet Revenge: The Wicked Delights of Getting Even.* New York: Harmony.

Beccaria, Cesare. 1764/1963. *On Crimes and Punishments.* Henry Paolucci, trans. Indianapolis: Bobbs-Merrill.

Bennett, Trevor, and Richard Wright. 1984. *Burglars on Burglary: Prevention and the Offender.* Aldershot: Gower.

Bentham, Jeremy. 1798/1973. *Political Thought.* New York: Barnes and Noble.

Berk, Richard A., and Joseph M. Adams. 1970. "Establishing Rapport with Deviant Groups." *Social Problems* 18:103–20.

Berkowitz, L. 1993. *Aggression: Its Causes, Consequences, and Control.* New York: McGraw-Hill.

Biernacki, Patrick, and Dan Waldorf. 1981. "Snowball Sampling: Problems and Techniques of Chain Referral Sampling." *Sociological Methods and Research* 10:141–63.

Bishop, Donna M. 1984. "Legal and Extralegal Barriers to Delinquency: A Panel Analysis." *Criminology* 22:403–19.

Black, Donald. 1993. *The Social Structure of Right and Wrong.* San Diego: Academic Press.

———. 1983. "Crime as Social Control." *American Sociological Review* 48:34–45.

Blackwell, Brenda S., Harold G. Grasmick, and John K. Cochran. 1994. "Racial Differences in Perceived Sanction Threat: Static and Dynamic Hypotheses." *Journal of Research in Crime and Delinquency* 31:210–24.

Blumstein, Alfred. 1995. "Youth Violence, Guns, and the Illicit Drug Industry." *Journal of Criminal Law and Criminology* 86:10–36.

Blumstein, Alfred, and Richard Rosenfeld. 1998. "Explaining Recent Trends in U.S. Homicide Rates." *Journal of Criminology and Criminal Law* 88:1175–1216.

Bourgois, Philippe. 1995. *In Search of Respect: Selling Crack in El Barrio.* Cambridge: Cambridge University Press.

Bourgois, Philippe, Mark Lettiere, and James Quesada. 1997. "Social Misery and the Sanctions of Substance Abuse: Confronting HIV Risk among Homeless Heroin Addicts in San Francisco." *Social Problems* 44:155–73.

Bowling, Benjamin. 1999. "The Rise and Fall of New York Murder: Zero Tolerance or Crack's Decline?" *British Journal of Criminology* 39:531–54.

Brantingham, Patricia, and Paul Brantingham. 1981. *Environmental Criminology.* Beverly Hills: Sage.

Brehm, S. S., and J. W. Brehm. 1981. *Psychological Reactance: A Theory of Freedom and Control.* San Diego: Academic Press.

Brown, Stephen E., Finn-Aage Esbensen, and Gilbert Geis. 1996. *Explaining Crime and Its Context* (2nd ed.). Cincinnati: Anderson.

Brownstein, Henry H. 2000. *The Social Reality of Violence and Violent Crime.* Boston: Allyn and Bacon.

———. 1996. *The Rise and Fall of a Violent Crime Wave.* New York: Harrow and Heston.

Brownstein, H. H., R. S. Baxi, P. J. Goldstein, and P. J. Ryan. 1992. "The Relationship of Drugs, Drug Trafficking, and Drug Traffickers to Homicide." *Journal of Crime and Justice* 15:25–44.

Bureau of Justice Statistics (BJS). 1993. U.S. Department of Justice, *Criminal Victimization in the United States.* Washington, DC: U.S. Government Printing Office.

CBS News 2000. Report transmitted on May 22.

Campbell, Anne. 1986. "The Streets and Violence." In *Violent Transactions: The Limits of Personality.* A. Campbell and J. J. Gibbs, eds. Pp. 115–32. New York: Basil Blackwell.

Cesar. 1997a. "Younger Arrestees in U.S. Favor Marijuana; Older Arrestees Stay with Cocaine." *Cesar Fax,* vol. 6, issue 26, July 7.

———. 1997b. "Marijuana Replacing Cocaine as Drug of Choice Among Adult Arrestees." *Cesar Fax,* vol. 6, issue 25, June 30.

Coleman, James. 1990. *Foundations of Social Theory.* Cambridge: Harvard University Press.

Collison, M. 1995. *Police, Drugs and Community.* London: Free Association Books.

Cook, Philip J. 1982. "The Role of Firearms in Violent Crime." In *Criminal Violence.* M. E. Wolfgang and N. A. Weiner, eds. Pp. 236–91. Beverly Hills: Sage.

———. 1976. "A Strategic Choice Analysis of Robbery." In *Sample Surveys of Crime.* W. G. Skogan, ed. Pp. 173–87. Cambridge, MA: Ballinger.

Cornish, Derek B., and Ronald V. Clarke. 1986. "Introduction." In *The Reasoning Criminal.* D. B. Cornish and R. V. Clarke, eds. Pp. 1–16. New York: Springer-Verlag.

Craig, Kellina M. 1999. "Retaliation, Fear, or Rage: An Investigation of African American and White Reactions to Racist Hate Crimes." *Journal of Interpersonal Violence* 14:138–51.

Cromwell, Paul F., Alan Marks, James N. Olson, and D'Aunn W. Avary. 1991. "Group Effects on Decision-making by Burglars." *Psychological Reports* 69:579–88.

Curtis, Richard. 1999. "The Ethnographic Approach to Studying Drug Crime." In *Looking at Crime from the Street Level: Plenary Papers of the 1999 Conference on Criminal Justice Research and Evaluation: Enhancing Policy and Practice through Research.* Vol. 1. Washington, DC: National Institute of Justice.

———. 1993. "Drug Distribution in Bushwick, Brooklyn: 1991–2." Unpublished manuscript.

Deci, E. L., and R. M. Ryan. 1985. *Intrinsic Motivation and Self-determination in Human Behavior.* New York: Plenum.

Decker, Scott H., and Barrik Van Winkle. 1996. *Life in the Gang.* Cambridge: Cambridge University Press.

Decker, Scott H., and Susan Pennell. 1995. *Arrestees and Guns: Monitoring the Illegal Firearms Market.* Washington, DC: National Institute of Justice.

Denton, Barbara, and Pat O'Malley. 1999. "Gender, Trust, and Business: Women Drug Dealers in the Illicit Economy." *British Journal of Criminology* 39:513–30.

Denzin, Norman K. 1995. *The Cinematic Society.* London: Sage.

Dietz, Mary Lorenz. 1983. *Killing for Profit.* Chicago: Nelson-Hall.

Dirks, Kurt T. 1999. "The Effects of Interpersonal Trust on Work Group Performance." *Journal of Applied Psychology* 84:445–55.

Dodge, Kenneth A., and J. P. Newman. 1981. "Biased Decision-making Processes in Aggressive Boys." *Journal of Abnormal Psychology* 90:375–79.

Dorn, N., and K. Murji. 1992. "Low Level Drug Enforcement." *International Journal of the Sociology of Law* 20:159–71.

Dorn, N., and Nigel South. 1990. "Drug Markets and Law Enforcement." *British Journal of Criminology* 30:171–88.

Drug Abuse Warning Network (DAWN). 1996. "Preliminary Estimates of Drug-Related Emergency Department Episodes." Report number 14. Washington, DC: U.S. Department of Health and Human Services.

Drug Enforcement Agency. 1997. *Changing Dynamics of the U.S. Cocaine Trade.* Washington, DC: U.S. Department of Justice.

Drug Use Forecasting (DUF). 1997. Quarterly Report. Washington, DC: National Institute of Justice.

Duffy, Michelle K., and Jason D. Shaw. 2000. "The Salieri Syndrome: Consequences of Envy in Groups." *Small Group Research* 31:3–23.

Dunlap, Eloise. 1991. "Shifts and Changes in Drug Subculture Norms and Interaction Patterns." Paper presented at the Annual Meeting of the American Society of Criminology, San Francisco, CA.

Eisenberger, Robert, W. David Pierce, and Judy Cameron. 1999. "Effects of Reward on Intrinsic Motivation—Negative, Neutral, and Positive: Comment on Deci, Koestner, and Ryan 1999." *Psychological Bulletin* 125:677–91.

Eisenhardt, K. 1989. "Making Fast Strategic Decision in High-Velocity Environments." *Academy of Management Journal* 32:543–76.

Ennis, P. H. 1967. Criminal Victimization in the United States: A Report of a National Survey. Washington, DC: U.S. Government Printing Office.

Feather, N. T. 1996. "Reactions to Penalties for an Offense in Relation to Authoritarianism, Values, Perceived Responsibility, Perceived Seriousness, and Deservingness." *Journal of Personality and Social Psychology* 71:571–87.

———. 1992. "An Attributional and Value Analysis of Deservingness in Success and Failure Situations." *British Journal of Social Psychology* 31:125–45.

Federal Bureau of Investigation (FBI). 1996. *Uniform Crime Reports.* Washington, DC: USGPO.

Feeney, Floyd. 1986. "Robbers as Decision-Makers." In *The Reasoning Criminal: Rational Choice Perspectives on Offending.* D. Cornish and R. Clarke, eds. Pp. 53–71. New York: Springer-Verlag.

Felson, Marcus. 1997. "A 'Routine Activity' Analysis of Recent Crime Reductions." *The Criminologist* 22:1, 3.

———. 1987. "Routine Activities and Crime Prevention in the Developing Metropolis." *Criminology* 25:911–31.

Felson, Richard B. 1982. "Impression Management and the Escalation of Aggression and Violence." *Social Psychology Quarterly* 45:245–54.

———. 1978. "Aggression as Impression Management." *Social Psychology* 41:205–13.

Felson, Richard B., and Steven F. Messner. 1996. "To Kill or Not To Kill? Lethal Outcomes in Injurious Attacks." *Criminology* 34:519–45.

Fields, A., and J. M. Walters. 1985. "Hustling: Supporting a Heroin Habit." In *Life with Heroin: Voices from the Inner City.* B. Hanson, G. Beschner, J. M. Walters, and E. Bovelle, eds. Pp. 49–73. Lexington, MA: Lexington Books.

Fleisher, Mark S. 1998. *Dead End Kids: Gang Girls and the Boys They Know.* Madison: University of Wisconsin Press.

———. 1995. *Beggars and Thieves.* Madison: University of Wisconsin Press.

Forgas, J. 1979. *Social Episodes: The Study of Interaction Routines.* London: Academic Press.

Freeman, Richard B. 1996. "Why do so Many Young American Men Commit Crimes and What Might We Do about It?" National Bureau of Economic Research, Working Paper Series.

Furst, R. Terry, Richard S. Curtis, Bruce D. Johnson, and Douglas S. Goldsmith. 1999. "The Rise of the Street Middleman / Woman in a Declining Drug Market." *Addiction Research*, 7:103–28.

Gabor, Thomas, Micheline Baril, Maurice Cusson, Daniel Elie, Marc LeBlanc, and André Normandeau. 1987. *Armed Robbery: Cops, Robbers, and Victims.* Springfield, IL: Charles C. Thomas.

Gervitz, Leslie. 1997. "Purer, Cheaper Snortable Heroin Floods U.S." Reuters News Service, December 31.

Gibbs, Jack P. 1989. *Control: Sociology's Central Notion.* Champaign: University of Illinois Press.

Glassner, Barry, and Cheryl Carpenter. 1985. "The Feasibility of an Ethnographic Study of Property Offenders: A Report Prepared for the National Institute of Justice." Washington, DC: National Institute of Justice. Mimeo.

Goffman, Erving. 1971. *Relations in Public: Micro Studies of the Public Order.* New York: Basic Books.

Goldstein, Paul J. 1985. "The Drugs / Violence Nexus: A Tripartite Conceptual Framework." *Journal of Drug Issues* 15:493–506.

———. 1981. "Getting Over: Economic Alternatives to Predatory Crime among Street Drug Users." In *The Drug-Crime Connection.* J. A. Inciardi, ed. Beverly Hills: Sage.

Golub, Andrew, and Bruce D. Johnson. 1999. "Cohort Changes in Illegal Drug Use among Arrestees in Manhattan: From the Heroin Injection Generation to the Blunts Generation." *Substance Use and Misuse* 34:1733–63.

———. 1997a. "Crack's Decline: Some Surprises across U.S. Cities." *Research in Brief.* Washington, DC: National Institute of Justice.

———. 1997b. "Monitoring the Decline in the Crack Epidemic with Data from the Drug Use Forecasting Program." Final Report to National Institute of Justice. New York: John Jay College of Criminal Justice.

Gould, Leroy 1967. "Crime as a Profession." Report to the President's Commission on Law Enforcement and Criminal Justice. New Haven: Department of Sociology, Yale University.

Gould, Roger. 1999. "Collective Violence and Group Solidarity: Evidence from a Feuding Society." *American Sociological Review* 64:356–80.

Gouldner, Alvin W. 1960. "The Norm of Reciprocity: A Preliminary Statement." *American Sociological Review* 25:161–78.

Granovetter, Mark. 1973. "The Strength of Weak Ties." *American Journal of Sociology* 78:1360–80.

Grasmick, Harold G., and Robert J. Bursik, Jr. 1990. "Conscience, Significant Others, and Rational Choice: Extending the Deterrence Model." *Law and Society Review* 24:837–61.

Grasmick, Harold G., Brenda S. Blackwell, and Robert J. Bursik, Jr. 1993. "Changes in the Sex Patterning of Perceived Threats of Sanctions." *Law and Society Review* 27:679–705.

Groves, W. Byron, and Michael J. Lynch. 1990. "Reconciling Structural and Subjective Approaches to the Study of Crime." *Journal of Research in Crime and Delinquency* 27:348–75.

Hackney, Suzette, David Ashenfelter, and Cecil Angel. 2000. "Crime Falls in State, U.S." Retrieved from www.freep.com/news/mich/crime8_20000509.html.

Hamid, Ansley 1998. *Drugs in America.* Gaithersburg, MD: Aspen.

———. "The Development Cycle of a Drug Epidemic: The Cocaine Smoking Epidemic of 1981–1991." *Journal of Psychoactive Drugs* 24:337–48.

Heckathorn, Douglas D. 1997. "Respondent-Driven Sampling: A New Approach to the Study of Hidden Populations." *Social Problems* 44:174–99.

Heckhausen, Jutta. 2000. "Evolutionary Perspectives on Human Motivation." *American Behavioral Scientist* 43:1015–29.

Heimer, Carol A. 1988. "Social Structure, Psychology, and the Estimation of Risk." *Annual Review of Sociology* 14:491–519.

Henslin, James M. 1972. "Studying Deviance in Four Settings: Research Experiences with Cabbies, Suicides, Drug Users, and Abortionees." In *Research on Deviance.* J. Douglas, ed. Pp. 35–70. New York: Random House.

Hindelang, Michael J., Michael R. Gottfredson, and James Garofolo. 1978. *Victims of Personal Crime.* Cambridge, MA: Ballinger.

Horswill, Mark S., and Frank P. McKenna. 1999. "The Effect of Perceived Control on Risk Taking." *Journal of Applied Social Psychology* 29:377–91.

Horwitz, Allan V. 1990. *The Logic of Social Control.* New York: Plenna Press.

Hughes, P. 1977. *Behind the Wall of Respect: Community Experiments in Heroin Addicition.* Chicago: University of Chicago Press.

Huizinga, David, and Delbert S. Elliot. 1986. "Reassessing the Reliability and Validity of Self-Report Delinquency Measures." *Journal of Quantitative Criminology* 2:293–327.

Hull, J. G. 1981. "A Self-Awareness Model of the Causes and Effects of Alcohol Consumption." *Journal of Abnormal Psychology* 90:586–600.

Inciardi, James A. 1986. *The War on Drugs.* Palo Alto, CA: Mayfield.

Inciardi, James A., Ruth Horowitz, and Anne E. Pottieger. 1993. *Street Kids, Street Drugs, Street Crime.* Belmont, CA: Wadsworth.

Irwin, John. 1972. "Participant Observation of Criminals." In *Research on Deviance.* J. Douglas, ed. Pp. 117–37. New York: Random House.

Isenberg, D. 1984. "How Senior Managers Think." *Harvard Business Review* Dec. / Jan.:81–90.

Jacobs, Bruce A. 1999a. *Dealing Crack: The Social World of Streetcorner Selling.* Boston: Northeastern University Press.

———. 1999b. "Crack to Heroin? Drug Markets and Transition." *British Journal of Criminology* 39:555–74.

———. 1998. "Researching Crack Dealers: Confessions, Dilemmas, Strategies." In *Ethnography at the Edge: Crime, Deviance, and Fieldwork.* J. Ferrell and M. Hamm, eds. Pp. 160–77. Boston: Northeastern University Press.

———. 1996a. "Crack Dealers and Restrictive Deterrence: Identifying Narcs." *Criminology* 34:409–31.

———. 1996b. "Crack Dealers' Apprehension Avoidance Techniques: A Case of Restrictive Deterrence." *Justice Quarterly* 13:359–81.

Jacobs, Bruce A., and Jody Miller. 1998. "Crack Dealing, Gender, and Arrest Avoidance." *Social Problems* 45:550–69.

Jacobs, Bruce A., and Richard Wright. 1999. "Stick-up, Street Culture, and Offender Motivation." *Criminology* 37:149–73.

Jacobs, Bruce A., Volkan Topalli, and Richard Wright. 2000. "Managing Retaliation: Drug Robbery and Informal Sanction Threats." *Criminology* 38:171–98.

Jacobs, J. E., and M. Potenza. 1991. "The Use of Judgment Heuristics to Make Social and Object Decisions: A Developmental Perspective." *Child Development* 62:166–78.

Johnson, Bruce D. 1999. Personal communication, November.

Johnson, Bruce D., Eloise Dunlap, Kathleen Boyle, and Bruce Jacobs. 1997. "Natural Transitions in Crack Distribution / Abuse." Prepared for NIDA, New York: NDRI.

Johnson, Bruce D., Ansley Hamid, and Harry Sanabria. 1992. "Emerging Models of Crack Distribution." In *Drugs and Crime: A Reader.* T. Mieczkowski, ed. Pp. 56–78. Boston: Allyn and Bacon.

Johnson, Bruce D., Terry Williams, Kojo A. Dei, and Harry Sanabria. 1990. "Drug Abuse in the Inner City: Impact on Hard Drug Users and the Community." In *Drugs and Crime*. M. Tonry and J.Q. Wilson, eds. Pp. 9–67. Chicago: University of Chicago Press.

Johnson, Bruce D., Paul Goldstein, Edward Preble, James Schmeidler, Douglas S. Lipton, Barry Spunt, and Thomas Miller. 1985. *Taking Care of Business: The Economics of Crime by Heroin Abusers*. Lexington, MA: Lexington Books.

Johnson, Eric, and John Payne. 1986. "The Decision to Commit a Crime: An Information-processing Analysis." In *The Reasoning Criminal*. D. B. Cornish and R. V. Clarke, eds. Pp. 170–85. New York: Springer-Verlag.

Jones, E. E., and T. S. Pittman. 1982. "Toward a General Theory of Strategic Self-presentation." In *Psychological Perspectives on the Self*. Vol. 1. J. Suls, ed. Pp. 231–62. Hillsdale, NJ: Erlbaum.

Kahneman, D., and A. Tversky. 1979. "Prospect Theory: An Analysis of Decision under Risk." *Econometrica*, 47:263–91.

Katz, Jack. 1991. "The Motivation of the Persistent Robber."In *Crime and Justice: A Review of Research*. M. Tonry, ed. Pp. 277–305. Chicago: University of Chicago Press.

———. 1988. *Seductions of Crime: Moral and Sensual Attractions in Doing Evil*. New York: Basic Books.

Khatri, Naresh, and H. Alvin Ng. 2000. "The Role of Intuition in Strategic Decisionmaking." *Human Relations* 53:57–86.

Kingery, P. M., B. E. Pruitt, and R. S. Hurley. 1992. "Violence and Illegal Drug Use among Adolescents: Evidence from the U.S. National Adolescent Student Health Survey." *International Journal of the Addictions* 27:1445–64.

Kirby, Kris N., Nancy M. Petry, and Warren K. Bickel. 1999. "Heroin Addicts Have Higher Discount Rates for Delayed Rewards than Non-Drug-Using Controls." *Journal of Experimental Psychology: General* 128:78–87.

Kirschenbaum, S. S. 1992. "Influence of Experience on Information-Gathering Strategies." *Journal of Applied Psychology* 77:343–52.

Kleinmutz, B. 1990. "Why We Still Use our Heads Instead of Formulas: Toward an Integrative Approach." *Psychological Bulletin* 107:296–310.

Klinger, David A. 1997. "Negotiating Order in Patrol Work: An Ecological Theory of Police Response to Deviance." *Criminology* 35:277–306.

Koester, S., and J. Schwartz. 1993. "Crack, Gangs, Sex, and Powerlessness: A View from Denver." In *Crack Pipe as Pimp: An Ethnographic*

Investigation of Sex-for-Crack Exchanges. M. Ratner, ed. Pp. 187–203. New York: Lexington Books.

Kroese, G. J., and R. H. J. M. Staring. 1993. *Prestige, Profession, and Despair: A Study among Robbers in Prison.* Arnhem, the Netherlands: Douda Quint.

Langer, E. J. 1975. "The Illusion of Control." *Journal of Personality and Social Psychology* 32:311–328.

Laub, John H. 1997. "Patterns of Criminal Victimization in the United States." In *Victims of Crime* (2nd ed.). A. Lurigiou, W. Skogan, and R. Davis, eds. Pp. 9–26. Newbury Park, CA: Sage.

Lauritsen, Janet L., Robert J. Sampson, and John H. Laub. 1991. "The Link between Offending and Victimization among Adolescents." *Criminology* 29:265–91.

Lawler, E. J. 1986. "Bilateral Deterrence and Conflict Spiral: A Theoretical Analysis." In *Advances in Group Processes.* Vol. 3. E. J. Lawler, ed. Pp. 107–30. Greenwich, CT: JAI Press.

Lejeune, Robert. 1977. "The Management of a Mugging." *Urban Life and Culture* 6:123–48.

Lejeune, Robert, and N. Alex. 1973. "On Being Mugged: The Event and Its Aftermath." *Urban Life and Culture* 2:259–87.

Lemert, Edwin. 1953. "An Isolation and Closure Theory of Naive Check Forgery." *Journal of Criminal Law, Criminology, and Police Science* 44:296–307.

Letkemann, Peter. 1973. *Crime as Work.* Englewood Cliffs, NJ: Prentice-Hall.

Lex, Barbara W. 1990. "Narcotics Addicts' Hustling Strategies: Creation and Manipulation of Ambiguity." *Journal of Contemporary Ethnography* 18:388–415.

Liska, Allen, and Barbara Warner. 1991. "Functions of Crime: A Paradoxical Process." *American Journal of Sociology* 96:1441–63.

Lizotte, Alan J., Gregory J. Howard, Marvin D. Krohn, and Terence P. Thornberry. 1997. "Patterns of Illegal Gun Carrying among Young Urban Males." *Valparaiso University Law Review* 31:375–93.

Lofland, John. 1969. *Deviance and Identity.* Englewood Cliffs, NJ: Prentice-Hall.

Luckenbill, David. 1981. "Generating Compliance: The Case of Robbery." *Urban Life* 10:25–46.

———. 1980. "Patterns of Force in Robbery." *Deviant Behavior* 1:361–78.

Lupfer, Michael B., and Bryan E. Gingrich. 1999. "When Bad (Good) Things Happen to Good (Bad) People: The Impact of Character Appraisal and Perceived Controllability on Judgments of Deserving-ness." *Social Justice Research* 12:165–88.

Lyman, Stanford. 1989. *The Seven Deadly Sins.* Dix Hills, NY: General Hall.

MacLeod, Jay. 1987. *Ain't No Making It.* Boulder, CO: Westview.

Maher, Lisa. 1997. *Sexed Work.* New York: Clarendon Press.

Maher, Lisa, and Kathleen Daly. 1996. "Women in the Street-level Drug Economy: Continuity or Change?" *Criminology* 34:465–91.

Maher, Lisa, and David Dixon. 1999. "Policing and Public Health: Law Enforcement and Harm Minimization in a Street-Level Drug Market." *British Journal of Criminology* 39:488–512.

Marongiu, Pietro, and Graeme Newman. 1987. *Vengeance: The Fight against Injustice.* Totowa, NJ: Rowman and Littlefield.

Matza, David. 1969. *Becoming Deviant.* Englewood Cliffs, NJ: Prentice-Hall.

McSweeney, Frances K., and Samantha Swindell. 1999. "General-Process Theories of Motivation Revisited: The Role of Habituation." *Psychological Bulletin* 125:437–57.

McWilliams, Peter. 1996. *Ain't Nobody's Business If You Do: The Absurdity of Consensual Crimes in Our Free Country.* Los Angeles, CA: Prelude Press.

Melburg, Valeria, and James T. Tedeschi. 1989. "Displaced Aggression: Frustration or Impression Management." *European Journal of Social Psychology* 19:139–45.

Mellers, Barbara, Ilana Ritov, and Alan Schwartz. 1999. "Emotion-Based Choice." *Journal of Experimental Psychology: General* 128:332–45.

Merry, S. 1981. *Urban danger: Life in a Neighborhood of Strangers.* Philadelphia: Temple University Press.

Mieczkowski, Thomas. 1986. "'Geeking up' and Throwing Down: Heroin Street Life in Detroit." *Criminology* 24:645–66.

Mihalopoulos, A. 1998. "St. Louis County Loses Population for the First Time." *St. Louis Post Dispatch.* March 18, A1, A7.

Miller, Jerome G. 1996. *Search and Destroy: African-American Males in the Criminal Justice System.* Cambridge: Cambridge University Press.

Miller, Walter B. 1958. "Lower Class Culture as a Generating Milieu of Gang Delinquency." *Journal of Social Issues* 14:5–19.

Mills, C. Wright. 1940. "Situated Actions and the Vocabulary of Motive." *American Sociological Review* 6:904–13.

Moessinger, Pierre. 2000. *The Paradox of Social Order: Linking Psychology and Sociology.* New York: Aldine de Gruyter.

Moore, Mark. 1977. *Buy and Bust: The Effective Regulation of an Illicit Market in Heroin.* Lexington, MA: DC Heath.

Nurco, David N., Ira H. Cisin, and Mitchell Balter. 1981. "Addict Careers: Trends across Time." *International Journal of the Addictions* 16:1327–1372.

Office of National Drug Control Policy (ONDCP). 1996. "Pulse Check: National Trends in Drug Abuse." Washington, DC.

Parrott, W. G., and R. H. Smith. 1993. "Distinguishing the Experience of Envy and Jealousy." *Journal of Personality and Social Psychology* 64:909–16.

Paternoster, Raymond. 1987. "The Deterrent Effect of the Perceived Certainty and Severity of Punishment: A Review of the Evidence and Issues." *Justice Quarterly* 4:173–217.

Paternoster, Raymond, and Leann Iovanni. 1986. "The Deterrent Effect of Perceived Severity: A Reexamination." *Social Forces* 64:751–77.

Paternoster, Raymond, and Alex Piquero. 1995. "Reconceptualizing Deterrence: An Empirical Test of Personal and Vicarious Experiences." *Journal of Research in Crime and Delinquency* 32:251–86.

Paternoster, Raymond, and Sally Simpson. 1996. "Sanction Threats and Appeals to Morality: Testing a Rational Choice Model of Corporate Crime." *Law and Society Review* 30:549–83.

Peterson, Elicka. 1999. "Moralistic Drug Robbery: Exploring the Intersection of Motivation and Justification." Paper presented at the Annual Meeting of the American Society of Criminology, Toronto, Canada.

Pettiway, Leon E. 1982. "Mobility of Robbery and Burglary Offenders: Ghetto and Nonghetto Spaces." *Urban Affairs Quarterly* 18:255–70.

Pirolli, Peter, and Stuart Card. 1999. "Information Foraging." *Psychological Review* 643–75.

Polsky, Ned. 1967. *Hustlers, Beats, and Others.* Chicago: Aldine.

Preitula, M. J. and H. A. Simon. 1989. "The Experts in Your Midst." *Harvard Business Review* 67:120–24.

Prus, Robert. 1984. "Purchasing Products for Resale: Assessing Suppliers as 'Partners-in-Trade.'" *Symbolic Interaction* 7:249–78.

Reidel, Marc. 1993. *Stranger Violence: A Theoretical Inquiry.* New York: Garland.

Reingold, David A. 1999. "Social Networks and the Employment Problem of the Urban Poor." *Urban Studies* 36:1907–32.

Rengert, George F. 1996. *The Geography of Illegal Drugs.* Boulder, CO: Westview.

Reuter, Peter, Robert MacCoun, and Patrick Murphy. 1990. *Money from Crime.* Santa Monica: Rand.

Reuter, Peter, and M. A. R. Kleiman. 1986. "Risk and Prices: An Economic Analysis of Drug Enforcement." In *Crime and Justice: An Annual Review of Research.* Vol. 7. M. Tonry and N. Morris, eds. Pp. 289–340. Chicago: University of Chicago Press.

Riley, K. Jack. 1997. *Crack, Powder, and Heroin: Drug Use and Purchase Patterns in 6 U.S. Cities.* Washington, DC: National Institute of Justice and the Office of National Drug Control Policy.

———. 1998. "Homicide and Drugs: A Tale of Six Cities." *Homicide Studies* 2:176–205.

Rosenfeld, Richard, and Scott H. Decker. 1996. "Consent to Search and Seize: Evaluating an Innovative Youth Firearm Supression Program." *Law and Contemporary Problems* 59:197–219.

Ryan, Kevin. 1994. "Technicians and Interpreters in Moral Crusades; The Case of the Drug Courier Profile." *Deviant Behavior* 15:217–40.

Sampson, Robert J., and Stephen W. Raudenbush. 1999. "Systematic Social Observation of Public Spaces: A New Look at Disorder in Urban Neighborhoods." *American Journal of Sociology* 105:603–51.

Sampson, Robert J., Jeffrey D. Morenoff, and Felton Earls. 1999. "Beyond Social Capital: Spatial Dynamics of Collective Efficacy for Children."*American Sociological Review* 64:633–60.

Sampson, Robert J., Stephen W. Raudenbush, and Felton Earls. 1997. "Neighborhoods and Violent Crime: A Multlevel Study of Collective Efficacy." *Science* 277:918–24.

Shaffer, John W., David Nurco, John C. Ball, and Timothy W. Kinlock. 1985. "The Frequency of Nonnarcotic Drug Use and Its Relationship to Criminal Activity among Narcotics Addicts." *Comprehensive Psychiatry* 26:558–66.

Sherman, Lawrence. 1993. "Defiance, Deterrence, and Irrelevance: A Theory of the Criminal Sanction." *Journal of Research in Crime and Delinquency* 30:445–73.

Shover, Neal. 1996. *Great Pretenders.* Boulder: Westview.

———. 1991. "Burglary." In *Crime and Justice: A Review of Research.* M. Tonry, ed. Pp. 73–113. Chicago: University of Chicago Press.

———. 1975. "Tarnished Goods in the Marketplace." *Urban Life and Culture* 3:471–88.

———. 1973. "The Social Organization of Burglary." *Social Problems* 20:499–514.

Shover, Neal, and David Honaker. 1992. "The Socially-Bounded Decision Making of Persistent Property Offenders." *Howard Journal of Criminal Justice* 31:276–93.

Siegel, Ronald K. 1989. *Intoxication: Life in Pursuit of Artificial Paradise.* New York: Dutton.

Simon, Herbert A. 1990. "Invariants of Human Behavior." *Annual Review of Psychology* 41:1–19.

———. 1979. "Information Processing Models of Cognition." *Annual Review of Psychology* 30:311–96.

Singer, Simon I. 1986. "Victims of Serious Violence and Their Criminal Behavior: Subcultural Theory and Beyond." *Violence and Victims* 1:61–70.

Skolnick, Jerome H. 1966. *Justice Without Trial.* New York: John Wiley and Sons.

Sluka, Jeffrey A. 1990. "Participant Observation in Violent Social Contexts." *Human Organization* 49:109–28.

Smith, Douglas A., and Craig D. Uchida. 1988. "The Social Organization of Self-Help: A Study of Defensive Weapon Ownership." *American Sociological Review* 53:94–102.

Spreen, Marius. 1992. "Rare Populations, Hidden Populations, and Link-Tracing Designs: What and Why?" *Bulletin de Methodologie Sociologique* 6:34–58.

Stansell, C. 1982. "Women, Children, and the Uses of the Streets: Class and Gender Conflict in New York City, 1850–1860." *Feminist Studies* 2:309–35.

Steele, C. M., and L. Southwick. 1985. "Alcohol and Social Behavior: 1. The Psychology of Drunken Excess." *Journal of Personality and Social Psychology* 48:18–34.

Stetkiewitz, Chris. 1998. "Surging U.S. Payrolls Show Economy Remains Robust." Reuters News Service, From Yahoo! Search Engine, February 6.

Sutherland, Edwin, and Donald Cressey. 1970. *Criminology* (8th ed.) Philadelphia: Lippincott.

Sykes, Gresham, and David Matza. 1957. "Techniques of Neutralization: A Theory of Delinquency." *American Sociological Review* 22:667–70.

Takahashi, Nobuyiki. 2000. "The Emergence of Generalized Exchange." *American Journal of Sociology* 105:1105–34.

Tedeschi, James T., and Richard B. Felson. 1994. *Violence, Aggression, and Coercive Actions.* Washington, DC: American Psychological Association.

Tidwell, Michael. 1992. *In the Shadow of the White House: Drugs, Health, and Redemption on the Streets of the Nation's Capital.* Rocklin, CA: Prima Publishing.

Tittle, Charles R. 1980. *Sanctions and Social Deviance: The Question of Deterrence.* New York: Praeger.

Toch, H. H. 1969. *Violent Men: An Inquiry into the Psychology of Violence.* Chicago: Aldine-Atherton.

Todd, Peter M. 2000. "The Ecological Rationality of Mechanisms Evolved to Make Up Minds." *American Behavioral Scientist* 43:940–56.

Topalli, Volkan, and Richard Wright. 2000. "Responding to Drug Robbery: The Role of Retaliation in Victim Decision-making." Paper presented at the annual meeting of the British Society of Criminology, Leicester, England.

Tunnell, Kenneth D. 1992. *Choosing Crime: The Criminal Calculus of Property Offenders.* Chicago: Nelson-Hall Publishers.

United States Department of Labor. 1998. Quarterly Report. Washington, DC: U.S. Government Printing Office.

Van Koppen, Peter J., and Robert W. J. Jansen. 1999. "The Time to Rob: Variations in Time of Number of Commercial Robberies." *Journal of Research in Crime and Delinquency* 36:7–29.

Van Mannen, John. 1988. *Tales of the Field: On Writing Ethnography.* Chicago: University of Chicago Press.

Walker, A., and Charles Lidz. 1977. "Methodological Notes on the Employment of Indigenous Observers." In *Street Ethnography.* R. Weppner, ed. Pp. 103–23. Beverly Hills, CA: Sage.

Walters, Glenn B. 1990. *The Criminal Lifestyle.* Newbury Park: Sage.

Watts, Duncan J. 1999. "Networks, Dynamics, and the Small-World Phenomenon." *American Journal of Sociology* 105:493–527.

Weaver, Frances M., and John S. Carroll. 1985. "Crime Perceptions in a Natural Setting by Expert and Novice Shoplifters." *Social Psychology Quarterly* 48:349–59.

Weinstein, N. D. 1980. "Unrealistic Optimism about Future Life Events." *Journal of Personality and Social Psychology* 39:806–20.

West, D., and David Farrington. 1977. *The Delinquent Way of Life.* London: Heinemann.

Wills, T. A. 1981. "Downward Comparison Principles in Social Psychology." *Psychological Bulletin,* 90:245–71.

Williams, III, Frank P. 1985. "Deterrence and Social Control: Rethinking the Relationship." *Journal of Criminal Justice* 13:141–51.

Wilson, William Julius. 1996. *When Work Disappears.* New York: Knopf.

———. 1987. *The Truly Disadvantaged.* Chicago: University of Chicago Press.

Wolfgang, Marvin. 1958. *Patterns in Criminal Homicide.* Philadelphia: University of Pennsylvania Press.

Wright, J. D., and Peter H. Rossi. 1986. *Under the Gun: Weapons, Crime, and Violence in America.* New York: Aldine de Gruyter.

Wright, Richard T., and Scott H. Decker. 1997. *Armed Robbers in Action.* Boston: Northeastern University Press.

———. 1994. *Burglars on the Job.* Boston: Northeastern University Press.

Wright, Richard, and Michael Stein. 1996. "Seeing Ourselves: Exploring the Social Production of Criminological Knowledge in a Qualitative Methods Course." *Journal of Criminal Justice Education* 7:66–77.

Ziegenhagen, Eduard A., and Dolores B. Brosnan. 1985. "Citizen Orientations toward State and Non-State Policing." *Law and Policy* 13:245–57.

Zimbardo, P. G. 1970. "The Human Choice: Individuation, Reason, and Order Versus Deindividuation, Impulse, and Chaos." In *Nebraska Symposium on Motivation* (vol. 17). W. J. Arnold and D. Levine, eds. Pp. 237–307. Lincoln: University of Nebraska Press.

Zimring, Franklin E., and J. Zuehl. 1986. "Victim Injury and Death in Urban Robbery: A Chicago Study." *Journal of Legal Studies* 15:1–40.

Index